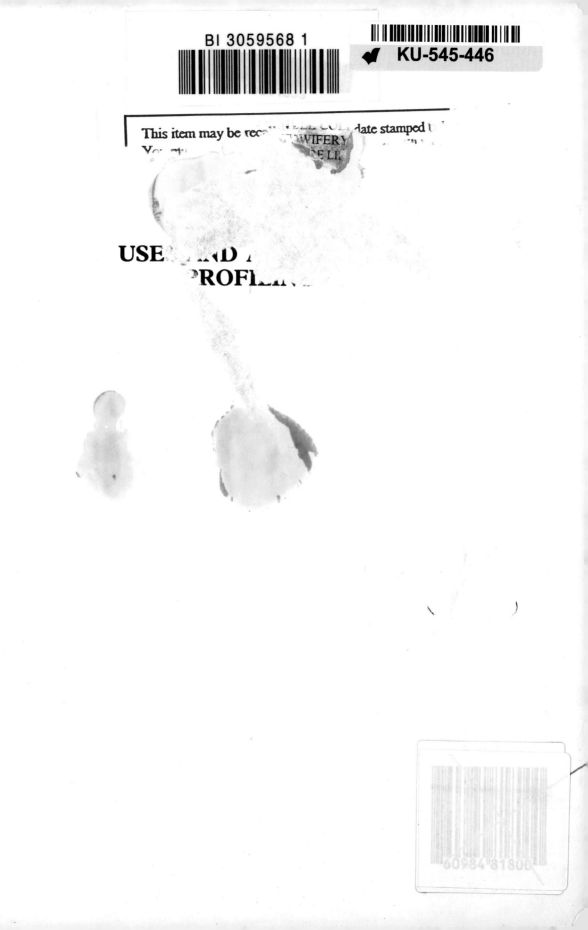

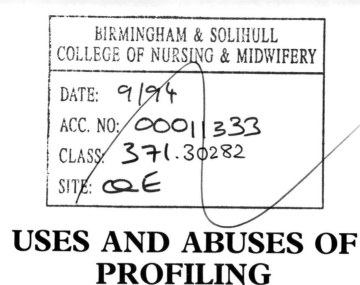

USES AND ABUSES OF PROFILING

A HANDBOOK ON REVIEWING AND
RECORDING STUDENT EXPERIENCE AND
ACHIEVEMENT

BILL LAW

National Institute for Careers Education and Counselling

Harper & Row, Publishers
London

Cambridge
Hagerstown
Philadelphia
New York

San Francisco
Mexico City
São Paulo
Sydney

First published 1984

Harper & Row Ltd
28 Tavistock Street
London WC2E 7PN

British Library Cataloguing in Publication Data

Law, W.
  Uses and abuses of profiling.
  1. Students, Rating of—Great Britain
  I. Title
  371.2'64   LB1117

  ISBN 0-06-318300-5

Typeset by Burns & Smith
Printed and bound by Billing & Sons Ltd., Worcester

To Peter Daws,

Who understood all this
long before profiling became a bandwagon.

CONTENTS

ACKNOWLEDGEMENTS

It would not have been possible to construct this handbook without the benefit of the development work on profiles, records of achievement, records of experience and client-centred reviews upon which it draws. I am particularly grateful to the holders of copyright listed in the Appendix for permission to include their material.

A number of colleagues have offered encouragement and help during the development of the handbook. I am especially grateful to George Pearson, formerly at the Schools Council, Helen Burchell at The Hatfield Polytechnic and Tony Watts at the National Institute for Careers Education and Counselling.

The handbook's critical, diagnostic and planning material has been used in a number of training workshops in various parts of the country. The interest, ideas and suggestions of participants in those workshops have been helpful influences in the development of the book.

My closest colleague on this project has been Pat Webster at the National Institute for Careers Education and Counselling. I am grateful, not only for her impressive secretarial skills in keeping the mass of much revised material organised and presentable, but also for her patient and supportive colleagueship.

Bill Law

INTRODUCTION

Profiling is a way of saying what is known about students; and is one of the means of determining which — if any — of our young men and women shall be selected for admission to an opportunity. This handbook invites a challenge to such a limited view of profiling. It also turns the decision-making process on its head by asking which — if any — of our profiling methods shall be selected for submission to our young men and women.

The handbook is arranged around the presentation of a range of profile formats used in secondary schools, colleges of further education and training programmes. The formats have been selected for their diversity. They are not all called profiles by their designers: some are called 'student- or trainee-centred reviews'; some 'records of experience' or 'of achievement'. The word profile is sometimes avoided for its connotations of pre-arranged and imposed structure. But the word is capable of use in a looser, more discursive sense, for example in journalism. It refers in this book to the whole range of methods of student portrayal which have been developed to replace — or at least to supplement — conventional assessment formats.

Among those conventional formats a principal dissatisfaction is with examination certificates and diplomas. But many of the formats examined in this handbook could also be used instead of or alongside other conventional forms of portrayal like school reports, cumulative records, references, *curricula vitae*, and personal appraisal and self-appraisal schedules (such as those issued by the careers service and employers).

PROFILES AND PROFILING

The word 'profile' refers to formats for portrayal. However, the words 'profiling', 'reviewing' and 'recording' refer to a more ambitious concept. This includes the tasks of putting marks on pieces of paper which represent 'knowledge' about people; the tasks of *saying what is known* — of making a product. But it also includes the tasks of gaining that 'knowledge'; the tasks of *knowing what is said* — of engaging in a process. The process is enmeshed with decisions about the intentions for the use of that knowledge; with problems for knowing what it is defensibly possible to say; and with dilemmas concerning access to, control of, and participation in the generation of that knowledge. Profiling is a complex art; it is certainly not just a matter of filling in forms.

THE HANDBOOK'S USES

This book can be read as an account of the 'state of the art'. But it is also designed to be used as a basis for action; to assist in the design of formats that can handle knowledge about students in ways which maximise the chances of intentions being realised, problems solved and dilemmas resolved. It invites its users to engage in a process of format development — whether by adoption, adaptation or creation — which is both critical and self-critical.

The material will be useful to:

- individual teachers who seek to develop profiling in their own subject or programme;
- working parties, teams and development committees engaged in recommending or implementing profiling programmes in their organisations;
- local groups of teachers who, as part of their mutual support and professional development work, want to include profiling as a topic on their programmes;
- people in advisory, consultancy or inspectorial roles who seek a resource for working with teachers on issues for profiling;
- tutors on teacher-training courses who seek workshop materials on profiling.

It will assist such people to come to the point where they can know:

- whether any of the methods represented here would be appropriate for use in the schools, colleges or programmes with which they are concerned;
- whether it would be most appropriate to consider adoption or adaptation, or whether the need is to design from scratch;
- where such a plan emerges, where to make a start, and in co-operation with whom.

STRUCTURE OF THE BOOK

No attempt has been made to minimise the size and complexity of the tasks. But it is also recognised that the time available for such development work is not infinite. The book has a structure, therefore, that invites the addressing of issues by stages. There are some parts which will prove of immediate use; and some a consideration of which can be postponed. Those decisions will be different for different users.

The opening chapter raises questions concerning intentions; such questions are basic to any profiling task. Chapter 2 leads to the identification of problems posed by intentions and closes with an invitation to the user to decide which of these he or she is going to address first. Although the chapters are cross-referred to each other, the basic design of the book is intended to make it possible to concentrate on one set of issues at a time. Different users will find different paths through the material. The total task is complex; the handbook is designed to help its users find a useful place to start.

Chapter structure

Each of the chapters is set out — with minor variations — in a sequence intended to enhance the book's usefulness to group as well as individual use.

An early *activity* is designed to stimulate responses to the issues raised in the chapter. Most of these activities are in paper-and-pencil form.

An *input* section summarises the main issues and ideas connected to the chapter topic. The material is briefly written so that it can be used as 'handout' material for group use.

An *examples* section sets out — with explanatory notes — a range of existing formats representing responses to the issues and problems posed in the chapter.

An *exploration* section revisits the themes with 'second thoughts' material comprising further argument and ideas. Ideas like those contained in these sections are likely to emerge from a group consideration of the material. Where there are abuses of profiling those abuses are often implicit in the issues raised in the second thoughts sections.

A final *action* section in each chapter reviews the main ideas contained in the chapter and suggests how they can be translated into action. The action may be task-group activity in training sessions. But it may also be incorporated into school, college or programme development work.

CHAPTER ONE

INTENTIONS FOR PROFILING

This chapter is designed to help examine:

- the basic features of profiles;
- your intentions for profiling;
- other possible intentions for profiling.

Dissatisfaction with conventional methods of portrayal is, in large measure, dissatisfaction with their capacity to convey what is known — and can be known — about students, with sufficient completeness, clarity and relevance to the purposes for which they are now necessary.

Rapidly changing societies deepen the dissatisfaction. The fabric of our lives is being transformed — particularly with regard to our work and our capacity to anticipate the future. In such societies it becomes more necessary to understand ourselves as individuals — what we each can do and what we each want. Selectors need more to go on for their changing purposes; teachers for theirs; and students for theirs.

What is new about profiles?

Many of the conventional formats for portrayal offer bald statements about students, without explaining why the statements are being made. Spaces for 'grades' and 'comments' do not invite contributors to say much about how the grade was achieved, or on what observations the comment is based. Conventional formats are usually structured by the dominant concerns of the organisations from which they come; in schools and colleges they are framed by the subjects on the curriculum. People are analysed by lines drawn across and around a timetable — subject by subject. Conventional formats tend to present students in terms of what has been retained; they offer estimates of acquisition of content. They do not necessarily say much about the individual way in which each student has gone about her or his achievements; with what skills, with what style, or with what motivations.

The formats shown in this handbook are designed to offer more scope for selectors, teachers, and students in one or more of the following ways:

- *By explaining what is being said* about students; by, for example, detailing events, behaviour and criteria; thereby making the portrayal more open to the gaze of its user so that she or he can relate it to her or his purposes more precisely.
- *By unpicking the basis for portrayal* and reassembling it so that it is not framed by the lines drawn across and around the timetable; offering the possibility that a single subject can be used as a basis for a number of different statements, that some statements will come from a number of different subjects, and that some bases for portrayal will be extra-curricular.
- *By making the portrayal more specific to the individual*; so that the user can gain some impression of the process by which a particular student relates to her or his experience, by saying something about the skills, styles and motivations which she or he has used.

They are, in a variety of senses, formats for the more manifest (more explained and more fully displayed) portrayal of students. To the extent that they are more manifest they are also more accountable — more likely, for example, to be challenged by students.

Some of the conventional formats referred to in the Introduction have such design elements. Reports which, for example, invite separate accounts of 'achievement' and 'effort' *begin* to provide for the explanation, reassembling and individualising of the basis for portrayal. To that extent they are rudimentary 'profiles'. No distinction between profiles and more conventional formats is entirely watertight. Some teachers, moreover, have used quite conventional formats to give more manifest and more accountable portrayals of their students; by, for example, carefully considering what should be set down in the section headed 'comments'. If contributors to profiles do not employ the same degree of thoughtfulness that some teachers have used on school reports, then profiles will deserve less — not more — credibility and use. The point about profiles is that they invite more manifest and accountable portrayal; they do not guarantee it.

Variations in profiling

While all the examples of profile formats in this book have, to some extent, each of the three features listed above, they each also have their own features. Those additional features have given profiling its extraordinary range and diversity. Differences between different profiling formats are often as great as differences between profiling and more conventional formats. Distinctive formats frequently owe that distinctiveness to specific intentions for profiling. And those intentions are informed by the whole spectrum of educational ideologies. Profiling has, as much as any piece of educational technique, been colonised by divergent ideologies. Although people may agree that profiling is a 'good idea', they may not agree in every respect about *why* it is such a good idea.

ACTIVITY

Your intentions

Why do you think that introducing or developing profiling in any organisation that you know about would be 'a good idea':

- What is wrong with what is already happening?
- What new outcomes might profiling produce, for whom?
- With these dissatisfactions and the pursuit of these new payoffs in mind, what sort of changes do you envisage profiling would entail?

Dissatisfactions: what's wrong now?

New outcomes: what new outcomes do you seek, for whom?

Changes: what therefore needs to be done?

How does your answer to these questions compare with a colleague's from the same organisation? Or with a colleague from a different organisation? How do you explain any differences?

INPUT

Possible intentions

There are no generally applicable 'right' or 'wrong' answers to questions about profiling intentions. They depend, as much as anything, upon what is already happening in the organisation, and upon what people think is wrong with what is already happening. New intentions are distilled from the comparison of unacceptable present realities and achievable future ideals. Both are relative!

Here are some such distillations of possible intentions. They each say something is wrong and improvement is possible.

For changing the *bases on which we present protrayals of students*:

- Traditional methods are too crude and global and mask individual differences. By *making fuller, more detailed use of the information about performance in subjects* that we already have, we can give more recognition to the fact that, at all levels of ability, different students are developing in different ways.
- Subject-based methods arbitrarily divide protrayals of our students. By *identifying a range of cross-curriculum 'core' characteristics*, which a number of teachers will have an opportunity to portray, we can offer a more rounded and whole impression of each of our students.
- Curriculum-based assessments are too limited; people are worth more than performance-in-curriculum can demonstrate — particularly in the examined part of the curriculum. By *extending the bases on which we portray our students* beyond the existing curriculum, and by paying attention to more than is traditionally associated with 'doing well' at school or college, we will make it possible for more of our students to show what they can do.

For changing the *bases for action by students*:

- Traditional methods of reporting and certification offer little incentive to many of our students. By *developing a form of portrayal which documents something of real worth* concerning each of them, we will provide them with motivation to sustained effort during their years at school or college.
- Traditional forms of assessment offer little information to the students about how and why they came to be assessed in that way. By *developing a method of portrayal addressed to the students*, which gives them detailed feedback on how they are being assessed, we will be offering them bases for changing what they do in order to bring them closer to where they want to be.
- Traditional assessments are part of the procedure by which schooling is given to students, their responsibility being limited to receiving what is given. By *developing a method of portrayal in which they are active participants — contributing to the record themselves —* we are acknowledging their responsibility for the way in which they are portrayed, and the fact that self-portrayal can be an educative experience.

For changing the *bases for action by teachers*:

- Traditional methods of recording and reporting give teachers very little to go on when they are required to give an account of their work, to help students, or to portray students to people outside. By *developing a more continuous and comprehensive bank of information about students* teachers will be providing themselves with a useful resource from which to draw impressions of how well the teaching and learning process is going, how to help students take their next step, and how to give a useful account of the student to others.
- Traditional methods of assessment are impersonal; students have little opportunity to discuss them. By *developing methods of portrayal which invite discussion in personal contact between teachers and students*, we are supporting teachers in their role as counsellors and giving them an opportunity of gaining direct feedback from students on the use students make of experience during their years at school or college.
- Traditional methods have shackled curriculum by forcing teachers to pay attention to what they know is going to be assessed. By *entering into a process of developing new criteria for assessment* we may release the curriculum from those shackles; we are also presenting ourselves with the task of re-examining the objectives of syllabuses and curricula — and of their relevance to the purposes of education and the lives of our students.

Some intentions may respond to present realities in your school or college more than others. Some may respond to your, and your colleagues', educational ideals more than others.

- The first three are useful to *summative* purposes; to seeking better ways of summing up a student at the end of her or his college experience. They could, for example, help employers and recruiters to training schemes to make selection decisions in a more informed way.
- The middle three are useful for *formative* purposes; to seeking better ways to help students get the best from their learning while still at school or college. They could, for example, help students to become more involved in and responsible for their decisions and experience.
- The last three are useful for *catalytic* purposes, to seeking better ways of bringing about changes, not only in the way in which schools and colleges assess students, but also in the way they develop curricula, relate to students, and make themselves accountable. In this sense, such purposes are formative to teachers in school and college — so that they can have a more informed basis for their decisions.

Within each cluster of three intentions, you may agree, the more cautious, easier-to-manage, and least threatening ones have been put first!

EXPLORATION

Second thoughts on intentions

Formative as well as summative?

Intentions for profiling can be clustered into the ways they provide bases for new action by different groups of people. Summative intentions provide new bases for action by selectors. Formative intentions provide new basis for action by students. Some analyses of profiles stop at that point. Indeed some analyses suggest doubts about whether summative and formative intentions can be realised on the basis of the same formats. Yet it is frequently the case that the assembly of summative material for public use gives rise to teachers asking why that material is not fed back to students at an earlier stage in order that they might use it for formative purposes. Some of the examples of formats given later in this book attempt to pursue at least some part of both sets of intentions, although their design frequently separates material which is intended for public consumption from material which is not (see Chapter 7, Proceeding with Caution?). That formative and summative intentions cannot be met from a single design is a proposition which has not yet been tested to destruction. In addition to separating material for 'public' and 'private' use, however, a problem for formative profiling is to ensure that students receive feedback at sufficiently frequent intervals that they can relate it to their immediate experience and use it as a basis for short-term actions. (For an analysis of methods designed for such 'continuous' or 'repeated' use see Chapter 7, Proceeding with Caution?)

Change by whom?

Summative *versus* formative analyses of profiling formats imply that it is selectors and students that must be helped to do what they need to do in a different way. The analysis of intentions given here challenges the idea that the *onus* of responsibility for more informed action lies wholly with selectors and students. Catalytic intentions provide bases for new actions by teachers. If the material on profiles is to become more relevant to the purposes of selectors and students, then the curriculum upon which that portrayal may, in part, be founded may also need to be changed. The very act of setting down clear criteria for portrayal is an act of redefining possible objectives for the teaching programme. The profiling of students is feedback to teachers on the use students make of that programme. Profiling can also help teachers do what they do in a different way.

Any scenario for profiling in a particular organisation can, therefore, be radically extended. Profiles originally introduced for summative purposes, can be identified as — and modified so that they can become — means of formative action on the part of the students. But, once in train, it seems likely that profiling will suggest to teachers that there are aspects of the school's, college's or programme's provisions which also need to be changed.

Cost-effectiveness of profiling

Developing a system of profiling is much more than designing a series of forms to be filled in. It entails deciding specifically why such a system is wanted; and it also entails adopting, adapting and developing materials that invite the kind of portrayal required. These are demanding-enough tasks. But profiling as a process entails more: it asks contributors to think in new ways about what the students are doing; and about what they themselves are doing.

It can be time and energy well spent. Introducing the idea of profiling can catalyse new thinking about curriculum, pedagogy, and organisation as well as assessment. But if teachers are already involved in a process of critically reviewing their work; if they are already involved in attempts to comprehend and talk with their students; if that is already leading to the development of more relevant and more accountable curriculum development and communication of information, why do they need profiling? An irony is that profiling seems likely to be introduced to organisations where such intentions are already being pursued, and less likely to be introduced where they are not.

Intentions and organisational priorities

Different organisations will contain different ranges of response to profiling. A great deal depends upon the way in which shortfalls in conventional methods are perceived. And that, in turn, is a matter of priorities — or values — in each organisation.

A consequence of this is that some approaches to profiling will not readily assimilate into some organisations. Canvassing radical and comprehensive intentions in conservative and traditional organisations can be hard work. Formats which have been enthusiastically developed in one organisation will not necessarily be so enthusiastically embraced in another.

Premature movement can lead to the digging of entrenched positions. But there is usually an intermediate step that can be taken; by first using formats which implement a less radical version of the intentions (see the Input section above), or by piloting a format on a limited basis and showing what it is capable of achieving. It involves finding a place to start. (Chapter 2 provides an analysis of a range of starting places.)

CHAPTER TWO

PROFILING PROFILES

This chapter is designed to help to identify and examine:

- existing profiling formats — as complete systems;
- features of such formats that help and hinder the pursuit of particular profiling intentions;
- starting points for action to adopt, adapt or develop methods which are relevant, reliable and valid.

Identifying intentions is largely a matter of decision-making, depending as it does upon the pursuit of some valued objective. Intentions spring from the answer to the question 'why?'. But the realisation of any intention depends for its implementation upon the ability to solve problems. While decision-making involves values, preferences and choices, problem-solving involves finding technical solutions. It answers the question 'how?'.

The technicalities of profiling address two recurring problems — of reliability and of validity. A portrayal is reliable if it does not contain within itself the tendency to distort the information it conveys. An elastic rule is an unreliable measure of length. A reliable portrayal will be consistent with itself. If there are variabilities in the portrayal of a person they will be because the person varies the portrayal, not because the portrayal distorts the picture of the person. A valid portrayal is one whose information is uncontaminated with unwanted influence; it is wholly about what it purports to be about, and nothing else. Some weighing-scales tell as much about the dishonesty of the vendor as they do about the weight of goods: they are invalid. A valid profile will portray the person and not the predispositions of its contributors or of its designers. Effective profiling methods involve finding methods which realise the intentions for which they are developed, but do so with acceptable levels of reliability and validity. Few intentions can be realised on the basis of distorted or contaminated portrayals of students. Questions for the critical examination of examples in this chapter are, therefore: Do they offer help or hinder the pursuit of valued intentions? Can they do so reliably without distorting what they portray? Can they do so validly without contaminating what they portray?

ACTIVITY

Relating methods to intentions

The following pages contain examples of profiling formats. They have been selected for their diversity. For the purposes of this activity you can include other formats that you know about, including any that may have been developed in your school, college or programme:

If you are working in a group, different members of the group could each take one example to work with. Examine each example critically — asking to what extent it meets the intentions you intend to pursue, and the extent to which it seems likely to do so without undue distortion or contamination.

Making notes under three headings will help with future developments of this approach to problems of portrayal. In relation to your intentions, identify:

- methods that appear to be particularly *helpful*;
- methods that appear to be *hindering*;
- methods which you can identify as necessary to your intentions, but which are *missing* from any of the examples you are examining here.

Before the examples there is an analysis of the formats, relating them to intentions. In that sense the analysis 'profiles' the profiles and gives an idea of where to look first. but it is a 'summative' profile of the profiles — identifying product features. And it cannot do justice to all the subtleties of their use in educational processes — particularly with regard to their use for curriculum development purposes.

When you have made your notes, try rewriting them as a series of 'problems' you have identified for solution: thus, 'These methods help (or hinder) the solution to the problem of . . .'; and 'These problems . . . are not addressed at all by any of these features'. There is a list of problems on pages 51–52 with which you can compare your own list.

EXAMPLES

Formats

The analysis relates each example to intentions:

Y   means 'Yes, this appears to be an intention of this system'.

Most systems are capable of adaptation and use to meet other intentions.

Intentions	P1: Personal Achievement Record (Evesham)	P2: First Year Home Base Curriculum Profile (Bretton Woods)	P3: Student's Personal Progress Record (Marple Ridge)	P4: Profile Report and Statement of Achievement (Comberton)	P5: School Leaving Profile (Schools Council, Wales)	P6: Record of Achievement (Ernulf School)	P7: Certificate of Vocational Preparation (RSA)	P8: Profile Folder (CGLI)	Other examples examined:
SUMMATIVE									
Make fuller, more detailed use of information about performance in subjects.	Y	Y	Y		Y	Y	Y	Y	
Identify a range of cross-curriculum 'core' characteristics for portrayal.	Y			Y	Y	Y	Y	Y	
Extend the bases of portrayal beyond the existing curriculum.	Y			Y	Y				
FORMATIVE									
Develop a form of portrayal which is more of an incentive to students than traditional assessments.	Y	Y	Y	Y	Y	Y	Y	Y	
Develop a method which addresses usable feedback to students on their performance while at school or college.		Y						Y	
Develop a method in which students can actively participate in their portrayal of self, to self and to others.	Y	Y	Y	Y	Y	Y		Y	
CATALYTIC									
Develop a more continuous and comprehensive bank of information about students for teachers.		Y	Y	Y	Y		Y	Y	
Develop methods which invite and support contact and feedback between teachers and students.		Y		Y	Y		Y	Y	
Enter a process of developing new criteria for assessment and new objectives for curriculum.									

Example P1:   *Personal Achievement Record*

The original is an eight-page plastic-covered printed logbook, measuring $3\frac{1}{2}$ by $6\frac{1}{2}$ inches.
Source: Balogh (1982) and Evesham High School.

	COURSE FOLLOWED			
	The following subjects have been studied during the last two years, at the levels shown.			
	Subjects	Level	Trial Exam Result	Stamp

EVESHAM HIGH SCHOOL
PRINCE HENRY'S HIGH SCHOOL

PERSONAL

ACHIEVEMENT

RECORD

SCHOOL ....

NAME OF STUDENT ....

DATE OF BIRTH ....

DATE OF LEAVING ....

Date...

Form Tutor...

The logbook is issued to any fifth former who asks the form tutor for it. When students believe they have mastered a skill or made an achievement they ask an appropriate member of staff to authenticate their achievement. If authentication is withheld, they can try again later. Students initiate, staff confirm.

The record is intended as an aid to interviews for employment. Employers were extensively consulted during its development, and help to pay for its costs. It is supported by notes addressed to staff explaining criteria and procedures to be employed; to students pointing out the value of the scheme, how it works and what they might record as an achievement; and to parents explaining the scheme and inviting them to join with the student in asking for a logbook.

LANGUAGE SKILLS

	Staff	Date	Stamp
1. Has legible handwriting			
2. Can write simple sentences			
3. Can read and understand a popular newspaper			
4. Can follow a set of spoken instructions			
5. Can use simple punctuation correctly			
6. Avoids elementary spelling mistakes			
7. Can write a personal letter			
8. Can give and take a telephone message			
9. Can accurately complete a driving licence application			
10. Can write a business letter			
11. Can make an accurate written report			
12. Can make a clear spoken report			
13. Can summarise accurately a notice or report			
14. Can understand simple instructions in a foreign language			
15. Can give simple instructions in a foreign language			

MATHS SKILLS

	Staff	Date	Stamp
1. Has a good accuracy in handling numbers			
2. Capable of performing everyday calculations in money accurately			
3. Able to understand everyday decimals including degrees of accuracy			
4. Able to handle fractions met in everyday life			
5. Understands money transactions such as wages and income tax			
6. Understands simple percentages			
7. Understands metric system of measure			
8. Understands English measures of length, weight and capacity			
9. Can interpret graphical information			
10. Is able to use a calculator			
11. Able to give a rough numerical estimate			
12. Has an understanding of V.A.T.			
13. Understands simple profit and loss			
14. Can read & understand time tables, wage tables & ready reckoner			
15. Has an understanding of banking procedures			

PRACTICAL SKILLS

		Staff	Date	Stamp
1.	Is aware of safety precautions in the home			
2.	Is aware of safety precautions in the workshop			
3.	Is aware of safety precautions in the laboratory			
4.	Can use correctly a domestic washing machine			
5.	Can iron correctly a shirt or dress			
6.	Can use correctly a domestic sewing machine			
7.	Is competent in basic cookery			
8.	Can use appropriate hand tools correctly			
9.	Can make 3 simple joints in wood or metal			
10.	Can understand a working drawing or pattern			
11.	Can express ideas in sketch or diagram form			
12.	Can choose and follow a route on a map			
13.	Can type accurately at 20 w.p.m.			
14.	Understands scientific terms in common use			
15.	Understands technical terms in common use			

PERSONAL AND SOCIAL SKILLS

		Staff	Date	Stamp
1.	Is normally and cleanly dressed for school			
2.	Is normally punctual			
3.	Has a good attendance record			
4.	Takes a pride in his/her work			
5.	Can work well without close supervision			
6.	Can work well as a member of a group			
7.	Can organise his/her work efficiently			
8.	Has played for school team			
9.	Can swim 25m			
10.	Is a regular member of a school club or society			
11.	Has attended a school residential course or expedition			
12.	Has helped at school social functions			
13.	Has taken part in school or year assemblies			
14.	Has had a position of responsibility at school			
15.	Shows a capacity for organisation and leadership			

PERSONAL ACHIEVEMENTS

ACHIEVEMENT	Staff	Stamp
(The student may enter here details of achievements, both in and out of school)		

PERSONAL ACHIEVEMENTS (continued)

ACHIEVEMENT	Staff	Stamp

A final page contains certifying signatures of the headteacher and the chairman of the governors.

Example P2:   *First Year Home Base Curriculum Profile*

In continuous development, the original is a folder containing, on typewritten A4 sheets with
'letraset' headings, a number of portrayals of the student's experience at school. One example of
an interim subject assessment is given here — for English — together with the form of a personal
profile (pages (v) and (vi) of this example).
Source: Bretton Woods Community School.

*Developed by teachers in each subject department, each subject portrayal is slightly differently laid
out, to accommodate the requirements of the way in which the subjects are taught; but each contains a
course outline, teacher's comments and a schedule to gain the student's responses to his or her work at
school.*

ENGLISH PROFILE: FIRST YEAR

| Name | Tutor Group | Year |

Course Outline

*The course outline specifies objectives, indicates content, and also indicates criteria for
assessment (e.g. 'careful presentation of written work including handwriting', 'accurate
spelling', . . . 'taking part effectively in discussion as a listener').*

(i)

Teacher's Comments

*This space occupies an A4 side and forms an ongoing written account of the student's
progress over the half-year. The page is divided into sections thus:*

- *writing;*
  grammar,
  spelling,
  handwriting;
- *reading;*
- *oral contribution;*
- *listening skills.*

*There is a final General Comment section for an overall 'summative' portrayal of the
half-year's work.*

(ii)

FIRST YEAR ENGLISH: INTERIM STUDENT EVALUATION

| NAME | TUTOR GROUP | DATE |

TICK THE BOX YOU THINK MOST APPROPRIATE

1. *MY HANDWRITING HAS*
   - ☐ IMPROVED
   - ☐ STAYED THE SAME
   - ☐ GOT WORSE

2. *MY SPELLING HAS*
   - ☐ IMPROVED
   - ☐ STAYED THE SAME
   - ☐ GOT WORSE

3. *MY PUNCTUATION HAS*
   - ☐ IMPROVED
   - ☐ STAYED THE SAME
   - ☐ GOT WORSE

4. *MY READING HAS*
   - ☐ IMPROVED
   - ☐ STAYED THE SAME
   - ☐ GOT WORSE

   AND EVERY MONTH I READ
   - ☐ MORE THAN TWO BOOKS
   - ☐ AT LEAST ONE BOOK
   - ☐ LESS THAN ONE BOOK

5. *THE STORIES I WRITE ARE*
   - ☐ VERY INTERESTING
   - ☐ BORING
   - ☐ QUITE GOOD

   AND
   - ☐ I LIKE WRITING STORIES
   - ☐ I DON'T MIND WRITING STORIES
   - ☐ I HATE WRITING STORIES

6. *THIS TERM IN ENGLISH I HAVE*
   - ☐ WORKED HARD
   - ☐ WORKED QUITE WELL
   - ☐ NOT WORKED WELL
   - ☐ IMPROVED A LOT
   - ☐ IMPROVED A LITTLE
   - ☐ NOT IMPROVED AT ALL

(iii)

THIS SECTION IS TO BE COMPLETED BY YOUR TEACHER

AS YOUR ENGLISH TEACHER I AGREE WITH YOUR EVALUATION OF POINTS

1 2 3 4 5 6 (Cross out numbers not applicable, add a comment if necessary)

7. WHICH SECTION OF ENGLISH WORK DID YOU FIND MOST INTERESTING?
EXPLAIN YOUR ANSWER _____

8. WHAT DO YOU NEED TO DO TO IMPROVE YOUR ENGLISH STANDARD?

9. IS THERE ANY OTHER COMMENT YOU WOULD LIKE TO MAKE ABOUT 1ST
YEAR LESSONS? _____

THIS SECTION IS FOR YOUR TEACHER TO REPLY TO ANY OF YOUR COMMENTS IF
HE/SHE WISHES _____

(There is more room in these panels on the original A4 sheet)

(iv)

An end-of-year 1st year English report is made on a format similar to that of the interim profile.

FIRST YEAR PERSONAL PROFILE

NAME _____   TUTOR GROUP _____   DATE _____

TICK THE BOX YOU THINK MOST APPROPRIATE

I ARRIVE AT SCHOOL
- ☐ EARLY
- ☐ ON TIME
- ☐ LATE

I AM ABSENT
- ☐ RARELY
- ☐ SOMETIMES
- ☐ OFTEN

I GENERALLY GET TO LESSONS
- ☐ EARLY
- ☐ ON TIME
- ☐ LATE

MY APPEARANCE IS
- ☐ VERY NEAT AND TIDY
- ☐ QUITE NEAT AND TIDY
- ☐ NOT NEAT AND TIDY

I WEAR PROPER SCHOOL UNIFORM
- ☐ NEVER
- ☐ USUALLY
- ☐ ALWAYS

IN MY TUTOR GROUP I HAVE
- ☐ MANY FRIENDS
- ☐ A FEW FRIENDS
- ☐ ONE FRIEND
- ☐ NO FRIENDS

I FIND IT
- ☐ VERY EASY TO MAKE FRIENDS
- ☐ QUITE EASY TO MAKE FRIENDS
- ☐ DIFFICULT TO MAKE FRIENDS

(v)

I GET ON   ☐ WELL WITH MY TUTOR
                            ☐ QUITE WELL
                            ☐ BADLY

MY TUTOR   ☐ HELPS ME WITH PROBLEMS IN SCHOOL
                            ☐ DOES NOT HELP ME WITH PROBLEMS
                              IN SCHOOL

WHICH SCHOOL CLUBS DO YOU BELONG TO? _____

HOW OFTEN DO YOU ATTEND AFTERNOON WORKSHOP? _____

WHAT HAVE YOU ACHIEVED DURING THE YEAR THAT YOU ARE PROUD OF? _____

WHAT DO YOU THINK ARE YOUR STRENGTHS AND WEAKNESSES IN SCHOOL? _____

WHAT ARE YOUR MAIN INTERESTS OUT OF SCHOOL? ANY OTHER COMMENTS? ____

(There is more room in these panels on the original A4 sheet)

(vi)

The whole document — comprising other subject assessments and this personal profile — is completed with an A4 sheet for both the 1st year tutor's report and parents' comments, both in blank spaces.

Example P3   *Student's Personal Progress Record*

The original is in a tag-bound card-covered printed booklet measuring 6 by $8\frac{1}{2}$ inches. A flyleaf addressed to students, parents and staff describes it as a 'constant source of information which is readily available to everyone'. The flyleaf also sets out a summary of the school's curriculum for the years covered by the record; the bulk of the booklet is given to subject assessment, two examples of which are given here for English and mathematics; the last pages of the booklet are given to the tutors' reports and students' diaries. Source: Marple Ridge High School.

MARPLE RIDGE HIGH SCHOOL

1983–84 Name_____ Tutor Group_____

PATTERN OF PROGRESS IN **ENGLISH**

			EXCELLENT	GOOD	REASONABLE	POOR	CAUSE FOR CONCERN	Subject Tutor's Comments	Parent's Comments
AUTUMN TERM	READING	Enthusiasm							
		Understanding							
	WRITING	Skill							
		Creative style							
	TALKING	Skill							
		Participation							
	LISTENING	Concentration							
		Response						Signature_____	Signature_____
SPRING TERM	READING	Enthusiasm							
		Understanding							
	WRITING	Skill							
		Creative style							
	TALKING	Skill							
		Participation							
	LISTENING	Concentration							
		Response						Signature_____	Signature_____
SUMMER TERM	READING	Enthusiasm							
		Understanding							
	WRITING	Skill							
		Creative style							
	TALKING	Skill							
		Participation							
	LISTENING	Concentration							
		Response						Signature_____	Signature_____

(i)

Each subject assessment is set out in a different form, to accommodate the requirements of the way in which the subjects are taught; but almost all contain spaces for a first, second and third assessment during the year (although some subjects give their assessments 'topic' rather than 'term' headings). Criteria vary between subjects, although there is an equivalent to 'attitude to homework' and 'interest and participation in classroom activity' included in almost all lists. All assessments include the 'excellent to cause-for-concern' five-point scales; all contain spaces for the subject tutor's report and the parents' comments; and almost all distinguish 'attainment' from 'effort'. All subject sections contain an outline of course content, objectives for and expectations of students; some subjects list work units with marks, some include unit-related graded test results.

MARPLE RIDGE HIGH SCHOOL

1983-84

Name _____ Tutor Group _____

PATTERN OF PROGRESS IN *MATHEMATICS*

		MID YEAR	END OF YEAR	1st ASSESSMENT DATE SIGN — EXCELLENT / GOOD / REASONABLE / POOR / CAUSE FOR CONCERN	2nd ASSESSMENT DATE SIGN — EXCELLENT / GOOD / REASONABLE / POOR / CAUSE FOR CONCERN	3rd ASSESSMENT DATE SIGN — EXCELLENT / GOOD / REASONABLE / POOR / CAUSE FOR CONCERN
	ATTAINMENT					
	EFFORT					
Attitude to homework						
Interest and participation in classroom activity						
Computational skills						
Ability to understand new mathematical concepts						
Ability to show methods used when presenting written work						

SUBJECT TUTOR'S REPORT

PARENT'S COMMENTS

ADDITIONAL COMMENTS

Signature _____

Signature _____

(ii)

The last pages of the booklet will, by the end of the year, contain two Group Tutor's reports (set out on page (iii) of this example) and some Student's Diary and Timetable pages, set out on pages (iv) and (v).

MARPLE RIDGE HIGH SCHOOL

1983–84

Name _____ Tutor Group _____

| EXTRA CURRICULAR ACTIVITIES AND RESPONSIBILITY |
| Tutor Group Involvement in the second half-year |

TUTORS COMMENTS

MERIT MARKS	
TOTAL No. OF SESSIONS HALF DAYS	
ABSENCES	
LATES	

PARENTS COMMENTS

Date_____ Signature_____

Date_____ Signature_____

_____ HEAD OF YEAR

(iii)

PUPIL'S PERSONAL TIMETABLES

NAME _____ TUTOR GROUP _____ SET _____

LESSON TIMETABLE

PD	MONDAY	TUESDAY	WEDNESDAY	THURSDAY	FRIDAY
1					
2					
3					
4					

HOMEWORK TIMETABLE

MONDAY	TUESDAY	WEDNESDAY	THURSDAY	FRIDAY

(v)

STUDENT'S DIARY PAGE

NAME _____ SET _____ TUTOR GROUP _____

WEEK BEGINNING MONDAY _____ 198 _____

MONDAY	
TUESDAY	
WEDNESDAY	
THURSDAY	
FRIDAY	

STAFF COMMENTS

PARENT'S COMMENTS

Parents Signature _____

(iv)

Example P4:   *Profile Reporting and Statement of Achievement*

The original comprises: self-portrayals (with accompanying notes and 'prompts' to help students use the system); 'Profiling Summary Sheets' which are issued to students at the end of the penultimate and final years of compulsory schooling; and a 'Statement of Achievement' issued at school-leaving. All are on typewritten A4 sheets.
Source: Comberton Village College.

Self Portrayal															
MY INTERESTS/LEISURE ACTIVITIES															
NAME					FORM										
Family Activities				Activities with Friends				Teams, Clubs, Societies				Helping Others			
Individual Sports				Relaxation				Going Out				Hobbies			

(i)

This self-portrayal also contains two other main sections headed (2) 'My Experience of Work' (with sub-headings on 'reading and writing', 'talking and listening', 'mechanical skills', 'creative skills', 'physical work', 'mental work', 'planning and organising', 'using numbers') and (3) 'My Character and Personal Qualities' (with sub-headings on being 'active', 'careful', 'co-operative', 'persistent', and on 'leadership', 'manner', 'appearance' and 'reliability').

Students are invited to locate themselves on the five-point scales accompanying each of the sub-heads (according to whether this is 'of no importance at all, I give no time or attention to this'; 'of slight importance, I give little time or attention to this'; 'of average importance, I give some time — at least occasionally — to this'; 'of definite importance, I give lots of time and attention to this'; or 'of the greatest importance, I spend every available moment on this').

Under each scale there is room for the student to write something 'brief but informative' about their involvements. They do not have to write something in every box.

Students are assisted by their tutors in producing their self-portrayals. They are also given 'prompt' sheets to help them to explore the width of their experience and self-knowledge. The sheets suggest the sorts of things students can record (see page (ii) of this example).

Experiences of Work

Here are some examples which may help you write your notes.

Reading and Writing
Reading novels; reading newspapers; reading factual books; reading about a certain subject; writing stories/poems; writing letters/diary; doing school work.

Talking and Listening
Talking about life; discussing issues; making speeches; acting; talking to friends; talking to adults; listening to others' views; listening to information.

Mechanical Skills
Mending things; building things; doing fiddly jobs; dealing with machines; working out how things work; driving.

Creative Skills
Designing things; painting/pottery; dressmaking; hairstyling; singing/playing instruments; dancing; making things for pleasure; growing things.

Physical Work
Gardening; carrying; sports; housework; decorating; keeping fit.

Mental Work
Thinking things up; considering problems; solving puzzles; developing theories; wondering why/supposing; academic subjects.

Planning and Organizing
Running a team/club; organizing disco/party; thinking ahead; making arrangements; looking after young children.

Using Numbers
Doing sums; using maths; accounting; finance; measuring; exploring science.

(ii)

Profiling — Summary Sheet (Fourth Year)

Name ....   Tutor Group ....Date ....

Interest/Leisure Activities

Experience of Work

Personal Qualities

Progress and Proposals

(iii)

Later on each student is invited to use the self-portrayal as a basis for completing this Profile Summary. There is more room for writing on the original A4 sheet.

Anything that will not fit into the four sections can be put on the back.

Students are invited to make judgements about themselves and to support those judgements with facts taken from their earlier self-portrayals.

The tutor reads the draft; and he or she may invite the student to add to the account — by suggesting things that have been left out or that the profile might need more detail.

The Profiling Summary is added to the subject reports to parents at the end of the year.

It is also intended that students use this sheet when they come to make their final statement of achievement in their last year at the school.

STATEMENT BY THE COLLEGE — TUTOR GUIDELINES

Attendance .... Punctuality ....

Interests/Leisure Activities
To be based on student's statement, a short comment from tutor.

Experience of Work
As with Interest/Leisure Activities, but it is worth specifically commenting on or endorsing those skills that the student has mentioned in his/her statement.

Personal Qualities
Tutors' comments should be positive, and should comment on areas such as: appearance, manner, initiative, sociality, independence, reliability, co-operation, thoughtfulness for others.

Progress and Prospects
This should be a series of statements about present progress and future prospects. Statements should be positive or constructive in tone. Areas to comment on could include: industriousness, output of work, fluency and accuracy of written work, oral skills, memory, observation, numerical skills, progress in particular subjects, reasoning ability. Potential for further education, suitability for A-level, O-level, vocational course/career aims should be mentioned.

Date .... Compiled by ....
                                                                          Tutor/Head of Year/Director of Studies
                                                        (iv)

During the fifth year students are invited to look again at their fourth year self-portrayal; and to decide what they want to add, subtract or change.

They can do this in discussion with their tutors.

A new version of the Profiling Summary is issued and completed by the student.

After discussion with the tutor a final version of the profile will be typed, and accompanied by a statement from the tutor — guidelines for which are set out on this page. (The original has more space for the tutor's statements.)

The two resulting statements are incorporated into the 'Statement of Achievement' which is intended to supplement — not replace — examination results. It contains only statements of positive achievement. There are four pages:

    1. Identifying information (name, leaving date, etc.) and head's signature.
    2. Signed statement by student, using the four headings on summary sheets.
    3. Signed statement by tutor, head of year or director of studies, using the same headings.
    4. Lists of examination results expected and already obtained.

The 'Statement of Achievement' is declared to be the joint property of the student and the school. The school uses it — instead of a 'secret reference' — to provide information about students, e.g. to prospective employers.

Example P5:   *School-Leaving Profile*

Still in development, this is a suggested approach to the production of a school-leaving profile with the aid of a computer. It is suggested that the document could be included in a stiffened wallet, along with a statement of external examination results.
Source: Schools Council Committee for Wales (1983).

Working groups of teachers assembled item banks for storage in a computer. The items are grouped as shown below on the right; each group has a 'bank' of at least five items hierarchically arranged.

ATTITUDE TO PEOPLE	● Relationships with other students/adults ● Organisational ability and leadership ● Other aspects of personality
ATTITUDE TO WORK IN SCHOOL	● Perseverence ● Presentation ● Organisation ● Degree of supervision needed ● Attitude to homework
ATTITUDE TO SCHOOL ACTIVITIES	● Enthusiasm for extra-curricular activities ● Type of activity ● Regularity of involvement ● Loyalty and commitment to school ● Attitude in class ● Trend in attitude to school
ORAL COMMUNICATION	● Participation in group discussions ● Range of topics ● Clarity of speech ● Personal conversation
WRITTEN COMMUNICATION	● Technical competence ● Vocabulary ● Reporting facts ● Style of writing ● Reading and understanding ● Extracting information
GRAPHIC COMMUNICATION	● Interpretation of drawings ● Production drawings
PRACTICAL SKILLS	● Manipulating equipment ● Measuring ● Understanding function and properties of equipment and materials

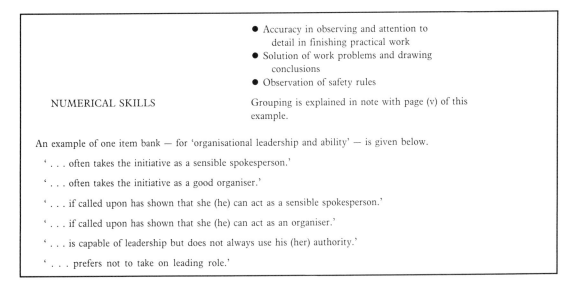

An example of one item bank — for 'organisational leadership and ability' — is given below.

'. . . often takes the initiative as a sensible spokesperson.'

'. . . often takes the initiative as a good organiser.'

'. . . if called upon has shown that she (he) can act as a sensible spokesperson.'

'. . . if called upon has shown that she (he) can act as an organiser.'

'. . . is capable of leadership but does not always use his (her) authority.'

'. . . prefers not to take on leading role.'

Other elements of item banks stored in the computer appear in the example of a printout given on pages (iii) to (iv) below.

Each department in school decides which item banks it can appropriately use. Departments, such as modern languages and music, can add to the item banks.

It is recommended that the nature of the assessment be explained to students; that they should be encouraged to monitor their own progress; that the use of the system should be accompanied by a programme of counselling; and that an intermediate collation of results should occur in the fourth year to keep students informed on the way impressions of them are being formed.

Subject teachers supply group tutors with codes for items for each student. More than one item can be selected from each bank. It is the responsibility of the tutor to eliminate contradictions and repetitions. The computer prints the profile as instructed by the tutor.

A sample printout is given on pages (i) to (vi) of this example.

TO THE READER

This profile belongs to .... who was a

pupil at the school from .... to ....

The information contained in this booklet is based on tests and continuous assessment conducted during the fourth and fifth years of secondary education. It is a consensus view of the pupil unless otherwise stated.

The document does not claim to be a forecast of a pupil's future development; a pupil may be very different after a year at work or college. It reflects attainment at the age of 16.

Headteacher's signature ....

Date of issue ....

(i)

NAME OF PUPIL _____   SIAN THOMAS   _____

ATTENDANCE — Year 4 _____ 97% _____

— Year 5 _____ 89% _____

Tutor's comments

Sian has shown a very good response to her school courses and to the varied situations she has encountered in school. She has demonstrated a degree of initiative and some self-assurance when these have been required and encouraged. When undertaking school work and extra-curricular tasks she has shown application and the capacity to work independently without being supervised. Not a natural extrovert by disposition Sian has, nevertheless, maintained very good relationships with fellow pupils and with staff, respecting their viewpoints and showing understanding. She has a number of varied and impressive interests which can be extended with great profit and we are grateful for the extent to which she has participated in school and community activities. Her community work is most impressive.

Sian has a very pleasant nature and is always cheerfully friendly in conversation. We wish her every success in her continuing efforts.

Signature of tutor ....

(ii)

Personal Qualities

Sian is able to form and maintain very good relationships with adults and pupils, although some encouragement is needed in the first instance. If called upon she has shown that she can act as an organiser but she prefers not to take a leading role.

Even in the face of difficulties Sian's perseverance and application are notable and very little supervision is needed to enable her to complete work. Homework tasks are completed regularly and usually satisfactorily.

When encouraged Sian participates reliably and conscientiously in school activities and she has shown loyalty and commitment to the school on many occasions.

(iii)

Communication Skills

Sian speaks readily in a small group but is more reluctant to contribute orally during class. She speaks clearly and usually correctly.

Sian can research and organise most information effectively and most written material can be read and understood. She has a feeling for language and uses an appropriate style of writing. Her command of vocabulary is good and she spells and punctuates with acceptable accuracy for most purposes.

Sian can interpret intricate plans, maps, patterns and diagrams. She can select the appropriate form of representation and is able to draw simple diagrams accurately.

(iv)

Practical Skills

Sian can perform tasks requiring a high degree of manipulative skill and shows a clear understanding of the function and properties of a variety of equipment materials and utensils. She is creative and practical in the solution of work problems and always practises safe habits.

(v)

Criteria of assessment in numerical skills are organised so that if students have mastered the basics, these are not separately listed on the profile, but summarised in one statement (the first in the example on page (vi)). Where the median range of skills is mastered (some of which are listed on page (vi)) then a further summarising statement appears, accompanied by a list of advanced numerical skills acquired. The method avoids taking much space to attribute low-level skills to advanced students. The numerical assessment is also different from others in this example in the way it attributes a level of performance in each skill; it ranges from A ('complete understanding . . .') through B1, B2, and C1, to C2 ('uncertain grasp . . .').

Numerical skills	
	Level of performance
Can understand and apply the four rules of number with confidence	A
Has full mastery of the use of decimals, fractions, averages and percentages in everyday situations	A
By estimation or suitable simplification can get an approximate answer and can use it to check detailed working	B1
Can use the common metric and imperial units in everyday situations	B1
Can use a basic calculator and use it appropriately	A
(vi)	

The design of the profile also provides for a contribution from the student who is invited to list personal interests and achievements, and school and community service — each with dates, descriptions and verifying signatures of people who know the activity has occurred as described by the student.

Example P6. *Record of Achievement*

In continuous development the original is in A4 typewritten format (with 'letraset' headings) comprising a range of assessments by staff and self-assessments by students. A covering note to the reader points out that the record is not intended to be used as a substitute for examination results or for confidential references.
Source: Ernulf Community School.

The front page (not given here) explains the purpose and content of the pre-vocational course to which the profile belongs.

Pages (i)–(v) and (vii)–(viii) of this example are completed by the student. There are three elements in the course: communication skills, social and life skills, and the world of work. The format of assessment for the first two is identical and is set out for one only — on page (iii). Teachers add their comments to those of the students on page (iii). The world of work assessment is on page (iv) and (v). Supervisor's assessment made while on work experience is given on page (vi).

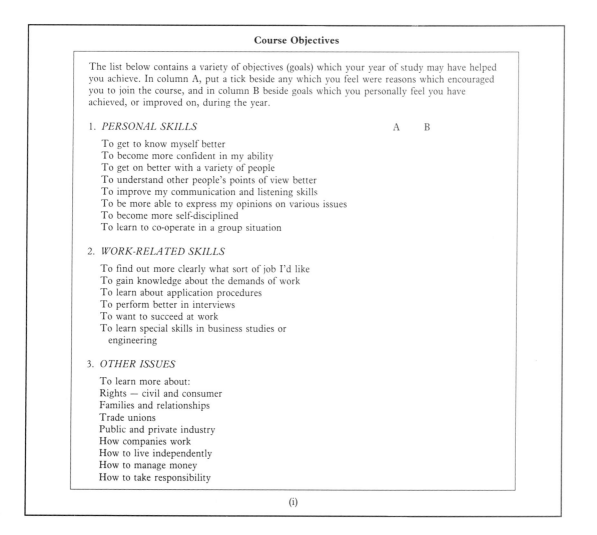

Course Objectives

The list below contains a variety of objectives (goals) which your year of study may have helped you achieve. In column A, put a tick beside any which you feel were reasons which encouraged you to join the course, and in column B beside goals which you personally feel you have achieved, or improved on, during the year.

1. *PERSONAL SKILLS*   A   B

    To get to know myself better
    To become more confident in my ability
    To get on better with a variety of people
    To understand other people's points of view better
    To improve my communication and listening skills
    To be more able to express my opinions on various issues
    To become more self-disciplined
    To learn to co-operate in a group situation

2. *WORK-RELATED SKILLS*

    To find out more clearly what sort of job I'd like
    To gain knowledge about the demands of work
    To learn about application procedures
    To perform better in interviews
    To want to succeed at work
    To learn special skills in business studies or
      engineering

3. *OTHER ISSUES*

    To learn more about:
    Rights — civil and consumer
    Families and relationships
    Trade unions
    Public and private industry
    How companies work
    How to live independently
    How to manage money
    How to take responsibility

(i)

The list overleaf is by no means exhaustive. In the space below, please add any other reasons you had for joining the course, and include any other goals which you feel you have achieved personally during the course of the past year.

REASONS FOR JOINING THE COURSE

GOALS I HOPED TO ACHIEVE

OTHER GAINS I HAVE EXPERIENCED

5th and 6th year studies

There are several ways in which a vocational course differs from the kind of courses offered in the Upper School. Can you describe the ways in which you have found this; and the differences, if any, this has made to your attitude towards learning?

(This page occupies a full A4 sheet in the original)

(ii)

Communication Skills

Course Content

(The aims, topics and modes of assessment are printed here in half an A4 page of type.)

Achievements

(This space, which in the original occupies half an A4 page, is used for separate reports by both the student and the teacher.)

(iii)

The World of Work

Achievements

(Completed by teacher)

Assignments

	Comp-leted	Grade
Job Specification		
Rights and Responsibilities		
The Red/Green Game		
How to Put Things Right		
'A Spot of Bother'		

Signed .... Date ....

(iv)

Work Experience — Student

Name of Employer

Place of Work

Describe the range of activities you were required to undertake whilst on your two-week placement.

Comparison between school and work

In what ways was your experience different when at work? Compare the following conditions at your placement to those you are used to at school and college.

	MORE	SAME	LESS
Level of noise			
Rest periods			
Physically tiring			
Mentally tiring			
Need for discipline			
Requirements of attitude			

Your own view

	VERY MUCH	REASON-ABLY	NOT MUCH
How much did you enjoy work experience and was it worthwhile?			
Were you given helpful initial training?			
How friendly were your colleagues?			
How helpful were they?			
Would you like this post permanently?			
How satisfied were you with your progress?			
Did it match your expectations?			
How pleased was your employer with you?			
Were you able to use what you had learned in school and college during the placement?			

Skills needed for this particular job

From the list below, tick each of the skills listed which you think were needed to succeed in the job you were doing:

Manual Skills

Strength

Self-confidence

Good manners

Friendliness

Tidy appearance

Self-discipline

Cheerfulness

A good telephone manner

Tact

Concentration

Initiative

Perseverence

Clarity of speech

Reliability

(v)

Work Experience Report

Name .... Placement ....

Period .... Work experienced ....

School ....

Attitude to work:

Effort/concentration
Attendance
Timekeeping
Safety
Discipline
Speed of work
Accuracy
Response to authority
Relationships with peers and others
Hygiene
Manual dexterity
Confidence
Initiative
Potential
General comments

(vi)

This format was developed by the employer; other employers use other formats.

Personal Qualities

Underline the words from the following list which you think are true of your own personality:

Easy-going	Relaxed	Adaptable
Extroverted	Ambitious	Generous
Thoughtful	Understanding	Patient
Hardworking	Sensitive	Persevering
Sociable	Considerate	Confident
Anxious	Co-operative	Lacking in confidence
Responsible	Modest	Reliable
Cheerful	Aggressive	Tidy
Quiet	Humorous	Popular
Shy	Competitive	Moody
Talkative	Noisy	Honest
Well-organised	Energetic	Punctual

Now, in your own words, write two or three sentences which you feel give a picture of your best qualities, including any which do not appear on the list above.

(vii)

Interest and Activities

Use this space to describe your interests and leisure time activities — these will range widely, and the sub-headings may help you to organise the information.

INDIVIDUAL INTERESTS, HOBBIES	SHARED INTEREST
TEAM OR INDIVIDUAL SPORTS	HELPING OTHERS/COMMUNITY
PART-TIME EMPLOYMENT	RELAXATION

(viii)

The remainder of the record is completed on one or more A4 sheets headed 'Final Summary of Achievement' by a teacher, from reports taken from subject staff and personal tutors. The reader is invited to compare the student's self assessment with this, and with the work experience supervisor's report. The pages are signed by the Head of Sixth and the Principal.

Example P7: *Certificate of Vocational Preparation — Clerical*

The system is in continuous development. The final certificate (pp.(v)–(vi) of this example) is on two printed sides of an A4 sheet.
Source: Further Education Unit (1982) and Royal Society of Arts (undated a)

Teaching objectives for the course are stated as criteria for assessment as set out on pp.(i–iii) of this example. Students are assessed to an agreed standard on each criterion — where appropriate, on the basis of test assignments. Students may, where necessary, repeat assignments until they reach the required standard. When they reach a satisfactory standard this is recorded on a master sheet (set out on p.(iv) of this example). The system may be supplemented by student diaries and log books.

The candidate is able to:

1. COMMUNICATION

    (i)   List, select and organise information using alphabetical order.
    (ii)   Use accurate spelling and punctuation.
    (iii) Draft simple letters and memos using appropriate layout.
    (iv)   Follow oral and written instructions.
    (v)   Use the telephone as an effective means of communication.
    (vi)   Abstract relevant information from messages and transmit this information in the appropriate spoken or legible written form.
    (vii) Complete a variety of forms.
    (viii) Use everyday reference books.

2. NUMERACY

    (i)   Add, subtract, multiply and divide with reference to whole numbers and money.
    (ii)   List, select, check and transfer numerical information accurately.
    (iii) Undertake simple calculations with reference to time.
    (iv)   Undertake simple calculations with reference to weights and measures.
    (v)   Undertake simple calculations using percentages.
    (vi)   *Undertake simple calculations involving commonly used fractions and their conversion to decimals.
    (vii) Take cash payments and give correct change.
    (viii) Read and understand commonly used tables, ready reckoners, diagrams and charts.
    (ix)   *Estimate with reference to time, space and quantity.
    (x)   Use a calculator with ability to estimate the answer in advance.

(i)

contd...

— contd... —

3. CAREER AND PERSONAL DEVELOPMENT

(i)   Establish and maintain working relationships with individuals and with groups.
(ii)   Carry out the task involved in all stages of the job selection procedures.
(iii)   Find and use appropriate sources of help and advice.
(iv)   *Examine his/her own interests, talents and values in relationship to the world of work.
(v)   *Understand some of the rights and duties of an adult in society.
(vi)   *Analyse one job in terms of the skills, training, qualifications, prospects, hours, conditions and likely pay involved and its availability and inter-dependence on other jobs.

4. HANDLING MAIL

(i)   Sort and distribute mail.
(ii)   Collate and check contents of envelopes.
(iii)   *Use a variety of equipment common in the mail room.
(iv)   Make postable packets and parcels with correct and legible addresses.
(v)   Weigh parcels and packages to calculate stamps needed.
(vi)   *Use franking machines.

5. RECORD KEEPING

(i)   Use alphabetical, numerical, subject and geographical systems of classifying material.
(ii)   Sort and sequence card indexes and cross-reference material for filing.
(iii)   Select information as required and transfer it onto or into dockets, forms, invoices, cards, books etc.
(iv)   *Write orders, bills and receipts.
(v)   Retrieve information as required from files and records.
(vi)   Identify the uses and sources of computer-based information.

6. OFFICE MACHINERY

(i)   Select and use as appropriate a range of reprographic equipment and materials including carbons, ink duplicators and photocopiers.
(ii)   *Use collators and staplers.
(iii)   Demonstrate familiarity with alpha and numeric keyboards.
(iv)   Type accurately envelopes and simple memos.

7. TELEPHONE AND RECEPTION SKILLS

(i)   Make and receive telephone calls appropriately to people and situations.
(ii)   Receive and record messages accurately and neatly and distribute them promptly.
(iii)   *Use simple switchboards.
(iv)   Give directions clearly and concisely.
(v)   Complete appointment books, message sheets and related records.
(vi)   Converse appropriately with waiting callers.

8. SECURITY, HEALTH AND SAFETY

(i)   State in simple terms the relevant obligations of the employer and employee regarding health, hygiene and safety.
(ii)   Identify hazards in work situations.
(iii)   Follow proper procedures in emergencies e.g. fire, theft, illness, accident.

(ii)

Items marked with * are optional objectives and criteria in this course.

ROYAL SOCIETY OF ARTS EXAMINATIONS BOARD
VOCATIONAL PREPARATION (CLERICAL) COURSE
Continuous Assessment Record

Date of Course: From .... To ....

Centre ....

CANDIDATES (Names in full, and block capitals)	Certificate Awarded	COMMUNICATION								NUMERACY									
		(i)	(ii)	(iii)	(iia)	(a)	(ia)	(iia)	(iiia)	(i)	(ii)	(iii)	(ia)	(a)	★ (ia)	(iia)	(iiia)	★ (xi)	(x)

Columns marked ★ on this version are optional objectives and criteria in the course. No certificate is issued until all compulsory objectives have been achieved. In each column ✓ indicates competence; X indicates competence not demonstrated.

(iii)

SAMPLE COPY ONLY

**Royal Society of Arts
Examinations Board**

ARTS AND COMMERCE PROMOTED

CATHERINE H. STACEY

has been granted this

CERTIFICATE OF VOCATIONAL PREPARATION (CLERICAL)

having fulfilled the conditions prescribed by the Royal Society of
Arts Examinations Board and having successfully undertaken a
Vocational Preparation Course in Clerical Skills,
the syllabus of which includes:

Clerical/Machine Operations

Language and Numeracy

Understanding Employment
Course duration
1st September 1982 to 11th May 1983

Chairman, Examinations Board

Examinations Director

*At the end of the course an external assessor checks students' work against the master record; and a word
processor is used to produce a certificate, an example of which appears here and on page (v) of this
example.*

COMMUNICATION, OPERATIVE AND MANIPULATIVE SKILLS
+++

HANDLING MAIL (incoming and outgoing)

Parcelling, addressing, weighing, stamping,
sorting and distributing mail.
Use of a post-book.
Use of a franking machine.

FILING

Using the filing systems which are commonly
available.

MACHINE OPERATIONS

Use of a typewriter for everyday operations,
such as typing envelopes , simple memos & forms.
Use of simple accounting machines, such as
ad-listers, tills.

COMMUNICATION (Numeracy)

Adding, subtracting, multiplying and dividing
with reference to whole numbers and money.
Undertaking simple calculations with reference
to time.
Adding, subtracting, multiplying and dividing
with reference to percentages and decimals.
Undertaking simple calculations with reference
to distance and weights and measures.
Accurate use of a ready reckoner.
Accurate use of a simple electric calculator,
with the ability to estimate the approximate
answer in advance.

CAREERS EDUCATION AND PERSONAL DEVELOPMENT
+++

The candidate has continued general education
and has received careers education aimed at
enabling the candidate to find, and ajust to,
work.

In addition the candidate has undertaken work experience allowing the practical application of elements of this course. For further details see the report from the candidate's own college.

DUPLICATING AND COPYING

Use of carbons, ink duplicators and photocopiers and hand collation.
Use of a spirit duplicator.
Use of a collating machine.
Use of electrical and heavy-duty staplers.

RECORD KEEPING

The maintenance of records using dockets, forms, invoices, books and stock record cards.
Using records as a source of information.

COMMUNICATION (Language)

Abstracting relevant information from aural and written messages and subsequently transmitting this information in spoken and written forms.
Completing records and forms.
Following instructions and directions, using enquiry skills and everyday reference books such as dictionary, telephone directories, travel maps and timetables.
Undertaking those additional functions generally relevant to office situations, such as checking, labelling and listing.
Drafting simple memos with accurate spelling and punctuation.
Reception skills, such as assisting clients, both in person and on the telephone, and receiving visitors.
Applying a knowledge of the geography of both the region and the UK generally in the work situation.

Example P8: *Profile Folder*

The system, in continuous development, is contained in an A4-size folder which is the property of the student, who should have access to it at all times. No entry is made without the student's agreement. The system leads to the award of a final certificate which incorporates the layout given on p(iv) of this example together with a written summary of the student's abilities.

The student's folder contains a 'student details sheet' indicating basic identifying information, and an outline of the route that the student is taking through the various courses and experiences. It also contains notes to the student explaining the use of the materials in the folder. Examples are given here of the three other components in the folder: (1) the logbook, (2) the reviews, and (3) the progress profile.

The scheme is supported by a handbook containing an explanation of the system, with examples of and exercises in its use.

Source: City and Guilds 1983, 1984

LOGBOOK

The logbook has 150 A5 pages. It is designed to be the basis of the whole system. It is intended for daily use — and no less frequently than once a week. It is also intended that all entries represent what the student has to say. The front of the book contains cues to reflection set out on pp(i) and (ii) below. Each series of questions is put in ascending order of complexity.

Things You have Done and Learned

- List what you have done today/this week.

- Which activity did you do best and why?

- Which activity have you learned most from?

- What was new, and did you take part in the planning?

- Are there any activities at which you need more practice?

- Do you think you made a good effort?

Working With People

- What responsibilities do other people have in the organisation?

(i)

- How have other people helped you?

- How have you helped other people?

- What difficulties you had when working with people?

Equipment and Materials You Have Used, Things You Have Produced, Services You Have Performed

- What equipment have you used?

- What materials have you used?

- What was being produced or what service was being offered?

- What have you learned about the equipment, product or materials?

- How was the quality of what you did assessed by (i) you (ii) your supervisor (iii) the client?

- What safety precautions did you take to protect (i) yourself (ii) others (iii) equipment?

Outside Activities

- Are there any other experiences you wish to be taken into consideration for your review and profile e.g. voluntary work, babysitting, paper round, hobbies, etc.

Personal

- This section is only for those of you who wish to use it.
  Is there anything else I want to write about the scheme or course?
  Is there anything else I want to write about myself?

(ii)

JOINT REVIEW

1. What are the main tasks or work areas covered in the last four weeks?

.... *These reviews are intended to occur no less frequently than* ....
once a month.

.... *Review sessions must not — it is urged — be disciplinary* ....
sessions.

.... *What is written in the review is intended to come out of a* ....
process of feedback to the student. The account is agreed
between the teacher and the student.

....
Where progress is made this is to be noted; and where special
.... *attention needs to be paid to future progress an agreement is* ....
to be worked out and a note made of it. The original appears
on two A4 sheets, giving more room for entries than is shown
.... *here.* ....

2. What has the trainee done particularly well? ....

....

....

3. After discussion, we have agreed progress has been made in: ....

but attention needs to be paid to: ....

....

....

4. The next month will be spent: ....

....

....

Trainee's Signature .... Date ....

Supervisor/Tutor Signature .... Date ....

(iii)

PROGRESS FILE

ABILITIES		EXAMPLES OF ABILITIES

COMMUNICATION	TALKING AND LISTENING		
	READING		
	WRITING		
	USING SIGNS AND DIAGRAMS		
	COMPUTER APPRECIATION		
PRACTICAL & NUMERICAL	SAFETY		
	USING EQUIPMENT		
	NUMERACY		
SOCIAL	WORKING IN A GROUP		
	ACCEPTING RESPONSIBILITY		
	WORKING WITH CLIENTS		
DECISION-MAKING	PLANNING		
	OBTAINING INFORMATION		
	ASSESSING OWN RESULTS		

The original is approximately 11 ½ × 16 ½ ". The left — with its detailed descriptions of specific abilities — is to be completed before the right. 'Bars' under each series of entries on the right are intended for 'hatching' to the level of competence reached. 'Half-way' hatching and 'box skipping' are discouraged. Teachers are encouraged to seek evidence for firm and continuous improvement.

The form is intended for six-weekly and final portrayals. It is completed in consultation with, and as a source of feedback to, the student.

It comes on 'ncr' paper so that the teacher can retain a copy.

The teacher will have consulted colleagues and relevant 'adults other than teachers' about progress before working with the student on the profile.

Where the 'basic' level has not yet been attained a note to that effect can be entered on the left. Where is is exceeded a star is entered in the extreme right-hand column.

On the final form a line is drawn to join up in a 'profile' of the levels of competence reached.

N/O = No opportunity to assess

Main Activities:

This box gives the reader an idea of the context in which the activities have been demonstrated.

1983 City and Guilds of London Institute.

PROGRESS IN ABILITIES

Can make sensible replies when spoken to	Can hold conversations and can take messages	Can follow and give simple descriptions and explanations	Can communicate effectively with a range of people in a variety of situations	Can present a logical and effective argument. Can analyse others' arguments	
Can read words and short phrases	Can read straightforward messages	Can follow straightforward written instructions and explanations	Can understand a variety of forms of written materials	Can select and judge written materials to support an argument	
Can write words and short phrases	Can write straightforward messages	Can write straightforward instructions and explanations	Can write reports describing work done	Can write a critical analysis, using a variety of sources	
Can recognise everday signs and symbols	Can make use of simple drawings, maps, timetables	Can make use of basic graphs, charts, codes, technical drawings, with help	Can interpret and use basic graphs, charts, technical drawings unaided	Can construct graphs and extract information to support conclusions	
Can recognise everyday uses of computers	Can use keyboard to gain access to data	Can enter data into the system using existing programs	Can identify potential applications for computers	Can construct error free programs	
Can explain the need for safety rules	Can remember safety instructions	Can spot safety hazards	Can apply safe working practices independently	Can maintain, and suggest improvements to, safety measures	
Can use equipment safely to perform simple tasks under guidance	Can use equipment safely to perform a sequence of tasks after demonstration	Can select and use suitable equipment and materials for the job, without help	Can set up and use equipment to produce work to standard	Can identify and remedy common faults in equipment	
Can count objects	Can solve problems by adding and subtracting	Can solve problems by multiplying and dividing	Can calculate ratios, percentages and proportions	Can use algebraic formulae	
Can cooperate with others when asked	Can work with other members of the group to achieve common aims	Can understand own position and results of own actions within a group	Can be an active and decisive member of a group	Can adopt a variety of roles in a group	
Can follow instructions for simple tasks and carry them out under guidance	Can follow instructions for simple tasks and carry them out independently	Can follow a series of instructions and carry them out independently	Can perform a variety of tasks effectively given minimal guidance	Can assume responsibility for delegated tasks and take initiative	
Can help someone to carry out clients' requests	Can carry out clients' requests under supervision	Can carry out clients requests without supervision	Can anticipate and fulfil clients' needs from existing resources	Can suggest realistic improvements to services for clients	
Can identify the sequence of steps in everyday tasks, with prompting	Can describe the sequence of steps in a routine task, after demonstration	Can choose from given alternatives the best way of tackling a task	Can modify/extend given plans/routines to meet changed circumstances	Can create new plans/routines from scratch	
Can ask for needed information	Can find needed information, with guidance	Can use standard sources of information	Can extract and assemble information from several given sources	Can show initiative in seeking and gathering information from a wide variety of sources	
Can receive advice about own performance	Can seek advice about own performance	Can assess own results, with guidance	Can assess own results for familiar tasks, without help	Can assess own performance and identify possible improvements	

Signed ....
(Trainee/Student)

Signed ....
(Supervisor/Tutor)

Name of Centre and Course ....

Period covered by this profile (dates) — start: .... **end:** ....

Mark III

INPUT

Problems for portrayal

A checklist of ways in which methods may or may not meet intentions is set out below; it is a list of problems for portrayal.

- Not all problems will apply to al! intentions; for some intentions some of the problems are not significant.
- Others might be particular problems for the sorts of intentions you have in mind.
- Some are inescapable; whatever your intention these problems are going to require to be solved if any reliability or validity is to be achieved.

All of the items complete the sentence 'If the intentions are to be realised then a solution must be found to the problem of . . .'

. . . providing material which is not restricted to the student's performance in the current curriculum.

. . . providing information which comprises reports of students' states of mind as well as records of events and behaviour.

. . . providing information about students' motives as well as students' performances.

. . . asking only for information which the sources of that information are in a position to provide.

. . . saying what an individual student's particularly 'strong' and particularly 'weak' characteristics are.

. . . offering comparisons between the individual student and other people.

. . . avoiding unnecessarily damaging comparisons.

Continued . . .

... avoiding the imposition of arbitrary frameworks for portrayal.

_____

... getting more than one perspective from more than one source on each of the students.

... involving people who are in the best position to contribute to each part of the portrayal.

... involving the students in their own self-portrayals.

... getting information and impression from a wide range of the students' activities inside and outside school or college.

_____

... employing language which will be understand by all its contributors and users in the same way.

... reducing the effects of personal bias in the portrayals.

... maximising the use of evidence and facts; and minimising the use of hunches and guesses.

... inviting portrayals which are independent of the personal preferences and attachments of the portrayers.

_____

... employing procedures which distribute control of information in an ethically defensible way.

... selecting the most appropriate formats, structures and layouts.

... linking portrayal procedures to other organisational processes such as counselling, curriculum development, and teaching-and-learning processes.

... ensuring that contributors and users are involved in the process in ways which they find valuable and manageable.

This checklist represents a possible list of problems for any person or group involved in the task of adopting, adapting or developing a system of profiling in a school, college or programme of activity. Its five sections pose different clusters of problem-solving tasks:

- Cluster 1: providing sufficient material of appropriate _content_.
- Cluster 2: providing appropriate but not arbitrary _comparisons_.
- Cluster 3: gaining material from appropriate _sources_.
- Cluster 4: avoiding the subjective use of _language_.
- Cluster 5: collecting, collating and disseminating material by means of appropriate _procedures_.

The word 'appropriate' is used in almost every line because what is to be done will depend upon what is intended. Different (ideological) intentions require different (technical) solutions.

EXPLORATION

Second thoughts on technical problems

Means and ends

No profiling system can do everything that everybody might want of it. Some can do hardly any! Many which, at first sight, appear not to meet critical requirements can be adapted so that they do. But, in any event, some requirements will be more necessary to certain intentions than others. For example, comparisons between students are not necessary to all profiling intentions. Comparison of a student's achievements with other achievements by the same student may be useful for some — but not all — intentions. Some intentions do not require that anything be said about the student beyond his or her performance in the existing curriculum. Others will be hindered by so arbitrary a limitation of portrayal. Many intentions can best be realised by having the student's own picture of him or herself included; some intentions cannot be realised at all unless that provision is made. The vital feature of one profile system may be rejected by another system designed for different purposes.

Professional or journeyman?

Do intentions spawn materials and techniques or do materials and techniques spawn intentions? The existence of profiling materials and techniques might have the effect of encouraging and supporting teachers in the expansion of their roles.

But making educational programmes dependent upon the existence of techniques and materials to occasion them seems rather limiting. Diverse as the range of profiling materials is, there is much more that *could* be developed. To make what is done wholly dependent upon the tools that already exist reduces the status of profession to that of journeyman. Professions are capable of re-jigging themselves with new materials and techniques that meet professional intentions. That means adaptation and development, as well as the adoption of existing tools.

On biting off what you can chew!

Embarking on the development of a portrayal system frequently involves more time and trouble than was originally envisaged. An examination of the 'Problems for Portrayal' checklist will suggest the extent to which almost every problem is intertwined with others; and suggesting a solution to one problem often itself poses two or three more. Seeking to confront the whole range of problems entailed by the development of a comprehensive system of portrayal, intended for a number of purposes, and to be implemented school-, college-, or programme-wide can be daunting — and might even lead to suffocation by overlapping complexities. It is avoidable — by setting clear boundaries around what it is that you or your group is taking on, stage by stage. That might mean restricting development work, at least initially, to the development of a system for use in one subject, one department or one element in the programme. It might mean concentrating initial attention on developing one part of what is ultimately intended to be a more comprehensive system. Or it might mean concentrating attention on the adaptation of any existing schemes by paying attention particularly to its greatest problems. This might, for example, involve adapting an existing scheme so that it has a more appropriate range of content; *or* employs a more suitable system of comparisons; *or* uses more appropriate sources of material; *or* is written in less subjective language; *or* follows more manageable and defensible procedures.

The activity suggested at the end of this chapter identifies the major clusters of problems in any existing systems of portrayal, and leads to the use of the remainder of this book as a resource for addressing that particular cluster of problems.

Of course, once the initial work has been completed it may well become clear that more work needs to be done — for other subjects, for other components in the system, or for other problems that the system poses. But the argument implicit in the structure of this book is that it is better to try to do one thing at a time.

ACTION

Identifying tasks

An examination of existing formats of portrayal — asking what helps and hinders and what is missing for the purposes of your intentions — will already have identified particular problems. This activity provides, if it is necessary, for the more systematic identification of those tasks.

Choose a 'short-list' of existing profiling systems which come closest to meeting the requirements of your intentions. Write the titles of those systems in the spaces at the head of the columns on the right of the analysis below. They can include examples given earlier in this chapter and other examples you are considering.

The spaces to the left of the analysis are for the identification of the problems that your particular intentions are going to entail. You already have notes about what — in regard to your intentions — helps, hinders and is missing from the systems you have examined. Some of those features will have to do with the technical problems of contents, comparison, sources, language and procedure — perhaps, in part, as they are set out in the checklist on pages 51–52. Write those problems for your intentions into the place on the analysis where they seem to fit best. There is a section at the end for problems that cannot be analysed in these terms. It might help to write each statement of the problem so that it completes the sentence stem 'If the intentions being considered are going to be realised then solution must be found to the problem of . . .'.

If you are working in a group the whole group will need to agree that these are the problems.

Write the titles of the systems being considered here

A	B	C	D	E	F	G	H	I

+ means this format contains methods which help solve this problem.

− means this format contains methods which hinder solutions to this problem.

0 means this format contains nothing which relates to this problem.

Problems concerning content

	A	B	C	D	E	F	G	H	I

Problems concerning comparisons

	A	B	C	D	E	F	G	H	I

	A	B	C	D	E	F	G	H	I

Problems concerning sources

Problems concerning language

Problems concerning procedures

Other problems

On considering your short-list you will be able to identify features which help (+), hinder (−) and are missing (0) in each format. If you are working in a group different parts of the group can take on the tasks of examining different examples of format. Enter the codes (+, −, 0) in the columns to show which formats relate to which problems in which way. The distribution of +, −, and 0 codes will give you an impression of:

● Where you have got some ideas for format to go on, which may need some adaptation, but come close to what you need for your intentions (+).

● Where you are going to have to do some radical adaptation if any of the existing systems are to prove of any use to your intentions (−).

● Where it looks as though you are going to have to search again to find something to meet a requirement of your intentions, or where you may have to do some original development work yourselves (− and 0)

Solutions to each problem will remove some of the distortion which gives rise to unreliability and some of the contamination which gives rise to invalidity, but each needs to be considered in relation to your intentions.

The remaining chapters in this book are arranged on the framework used in the analysis. So this exercise might suggest where first to go in your task. The chapters are arranged thus:

CHAPTER THREE

TELLING WHAT?

This chapter is designed to help identify:

- how far the material for portrayal should relate to existing curricular concerns;
- how far it should comprise records of events and behaviour, or whether it must contain generalised statements and interpretations of inner states;
- whether or not it should — or must — depend only on what teachers know about students;
- whether it is to portray information and impressions limited to knowledge of student performance, or whether material about student motivations is also important.

Talking about students can involve portraying a wide range of different sorts of information and impression.

- Accounts of *events*; for example, of tasks accomplished, courses attended, experience engaged in.
- Descriptions of *physical skills and dispositions*; for example, of appearance, health, manual skills.
- Assessments of *mental abilities*; such as ability with 'language', 'number', 'problem solving'.
- General pictures of *personal dispositions*; the way in which each student puts an individual 'thumbprint' on much of what he or she does: students are, for example, said to be 'confident' or to have 'leadership' or to be 'reliable'.
- Impressions of *motivations*; of what interests and attracts the student, of likes and interests, even of aspirations and yearnings.

Yet no profile can set down all the information and impression that might be told. All portrayals are partial. Much depends on what the material is intended for. Such intentions can be stated by saying that the material is *for* a particular audience *so that* they can do something (see Chapter 1, Intentions for Profiling).

ACTIVITY

Uses of portrayal

This is a first examination of the sorts of information you have in mind for a profile. It can be used individually and for group-comparison and discussion.

The main intentions being considered for profiling are . . .
for . . .
so that . . .
for . . .
so that . . .
for . . .
so that . . .

What does that mean in relation to particular students known to you? Think of students for whom your purposes are particularly relevant: what information and impression about each of the students do you consider would need to be portrayed on a profile in order to serve those purposes?

Student 1	Student 2
Student 3	Student 4

The following section will help to re-examine, supplement and analyse the content of information you have in mind.

INPUT

What might go on a profile?

The panel below analyses the various types of information and impression which might appear on a profile. The categories are not — cannot be — absolutely separate from each other.

Record of experiences and activities

- *Courses attended*: topics studied, tasks accomplished, learning acquired, results (e.g. qualifications) obtained.

- *Extra-curricular experience*: activities engaged in, roles and relationships experienced, learning acquired.

- *School- or college-sponsored off-site experience* (e.g. work experience, voluntary work placements, residential courses, etc.): people contacted, places been, roles occupied, things done, learning acquired.

- *Other out-of-school or -college experience* (e.g. part-time jobs held, club memberships, leisure pursuits, etc.): people contacted, places been, things done, learning acquired.

Physical skills and dispositions displayed in one or more activities

- Health (e.g. allergies, sight, hearing, etc.)

- Physique (height, etc.)

- Speech

- Strength

- Dexterity

- Co-ordination

- Appearance

Mental abilities displayed in one or more activities

- *Verbal comprehension* — to gain accurate impressions from speech and writing.

- *Word fluency* — to give accurate expression through speech and writing.

- *Numeracy* — to understand and express ideas accurately through numbers.
- *Spatial ability* — to understand the relationship between shapes and objects in two or three dimensions (e.g. with patterns, maps, diagrams, objects).
- *Memory* — to retain and recall material accurately.
- *Perceptiveness* — to locate and identify things in their details precisely.
- *Reasoning ability* — validly to order and analyse knowledge and to move from the known to the unknown by making new and valid conclusions.
- *Originality* — to produce a flow of new, useful and unexpected ideas.

Personal and social dispositions displayed or disclosed

- *Activity* level; e.g. effort, energy, drive, vigour.
- *Carefulness*; e.g. thoroughness, attention to detail, precision, caution.
- *Co-operation*; e.g. adaptability, open-mindedness, group-dependence, courtesy.
- *Dominance*; e.g. assertiveness, initiative, responsibility, leadership.
- *Resilience*; e.g. stress handling, calmness, consistency, persistence.
- *Self-sufficiency*; e.g. resourcefulness, independence, self-directedness.
- *Sensitivity*; e.g. responsiveness, empathy, tact, affective insights.
- *Sociability*; e.g. easy-goingness, good humour, participation with others, unreservedness, spontaneity.
- *Trustworthiness*; e.g. honesty, punctuality, reliability, conformity, conscientiousness, self-discipline.

Needs and wants disclosed or inferred

- Towards what is *practical*; e.g. what offers concrete, tangible, material or useful rewards.
- For *security*; e.g. what offers safe, predictable, stable, protected or structured situations.
- Towards *social contact*; e.g. what offers opportunities for companionship with, and from, others.
- In search of *attention*; e.g. what offers acknowledgement by others, prestige, esteem, status or applause.
- For *influence*; e.g. what offers opportunities for gaining personal responsibility, and the power to get results.
- For *curiosity*; e.g. what offers opportunities for discovery, knowledge, understanding.
- Towards what is *aesthetic*; e.g. what offers appreciation of the arts or the quality of the environment.
- For *achievement*; e.g. what offers opportunities for successful competition, self-realisation, self-fulfilment.

- Some types of information relate closely to the concerns of existing curricula; some concern themselves with portraying what the curriculum may not be designed to develop.
- Some are a matter for factual observations and reports of verifiable events and behaviour; some require that generalised judgements and interpretations are given as opinions.
- Some refer to things that teachers can know about; some refer to things that teachers have little opportunity to form any impression on; some are things that only the students could validly portray.
- Some refer to what students have to offer as performance (skills, capacities and competencies); others refer to what students seek as motives (drives, aspirations, needs and wants).

EXPLORATION

Second thoughts on content

Curriculum and profiling

You may take the view that the portrayal should concern itself only with what the current curriculum is designed to identify and develop in students. That has the virtue of making assessment dependent upon curriculum (many have argued that curriculum has, in the past, been too independent upon assessment — a case of examination-tails wagging curriculum-dogs!). But, for some intentions, restricting the content of portrayal only to what the current curriculum is offering will be too arbitrarily restrictive. If, for example, students are being invited to use that portrayal as a source of feedback for the formative purposes of developing future plans, then information and impression about themselves which relates only to existing curriculum may be too narrow. And, if the intention is to catalyse new development in the school or college's curriculum, then broadening the range of content to be included in the portrayal might prove catalytic to further curriculum development (see Chapter 1, Intentions for Profiling).

Facts and interpretations

It may be thought desirable to stay with factual accounts of events and verifiable descriptions of observed characteristics, but gaining the range of material required for some profiling intentions requires an unmanageably large collection of such reports. Some specific observations may have to be condensed into general interpretations and impressions of the students. Where that is done it is important that the profile makes it clear what is being reported as a specific event or behaviour, and what is being recorded as a general interpretation or impression of the person (Chapter 6, Word Perfect?, examines some techniques for identifying this distinction).

Content and sources

The fact that you think that a particular sort of content should appear on the portrayal does not guarantee that you will have valid and reliable sources for that material. Different people know students in different settings and are therefore able to give only certain sorts of information. Some may resist being asked to portray what they have little opportunity to observe, or what seems to have little relevance to their purposes. The more dangerous case is where sources feel obliged to give some kind of answer to the enquiry which has been directed at them but which they are not in a good position to answer. Decisions about content involve decisions about sources — who is in a best position to say what about a student? There are some things that teachers are in no position to report; some that could only be observed in settings outside school; and some that only the students would be in a position to report. (Chapter 5, Says Who?, examines techniques for employing a sample of sources in gaining portrayals and self-portrayals of students.)

Portrayal and organisational culture

Organisations can have a dominant culture. What have been called 'Comanche' schools and colleges celebrate the discovery in their students of evidence for 'competitiveness', 'dominance' and 'self-sufficiency', while 'Pueblo' organisations honour the documentation of 'co-operativeness', 'creativity' and 'spontaneity'. Such cultures can colour the transmission of information about students: by making it more likely that certain kinds of information will be sought; by influencing which students have which sorts of ascriptions made to them; and by giving ambiguous words significantly different connotations — the word 'reliable' can easily mean something different in Comanche and Pueblo cultures! The effects of such distortion can be minimised: by getting information from a variety of sources — including sources outside the school or college (see Chapter 5); and also by wording the profile in a way which neutralises the values which the organisation arbitrarily places on certain characteristics (see Chapter 6).

Capacities and motives

There are some statements which are obviously of concern to those who want to know what students can do — statements of performance, skill, capacity and competence. But skills come attached to people, and people are more than their skills; they also have motives.

Motives (such as interests, aspirations and yearnings) are difficult to portray — other people's and one's own. But knowledge of motives may be some of the most important information about self that needs to be examined and understood. They put steam into a person. When people fail to achieve what others want of them it is not always because they cannot do it, it is quite often because they see no point in it — it has no pay-off *for them*. Understanding the rewards someone wants from life is an important way of understanding that person.

It is extremely doubtful whether a student should be required to disclose information about his or her motives on a public record (if they choose to do so, it is another matter). Chapter 7, Proceeding with Caution?, examines techniques for portraying motives in a profiling system, but in a way which leaves control of the information and impression in the hands of the student.

ACTION

Planning content

How far can you now go in planning the content of the profile? How far can you agree with colleagues on any of the following issues?

- What information and impression about students should the portrayal contain?
  . . . how dependent upon existing curricular concerns?
  . . . how limited to statements about performance, skills, capacities and competencies?
- How are the various bits of information and impression to be framed on the portrayal?
  What parts of the portrayal will
  . . . use descriptions of behaviour and events?
  . . . ask for more generalised interpretations based on repeated observations?
  . . . require that statements are made about inner states (such as personal and social dispositions or motives)?
- Where can you get any of that material?
  . . . from subject and course teachers?
  . . . more broadly across the curriculum?
  . . . from outside the school or college?
  . . . from the students?

CHAPTER FOUR

COMPARED TO WHAT?

This chapter is designed to help examine:

- methods for comparing a student's 'strengths' with 'weaknesses';
- methods for comparing one person with others;
- methods that avoid comparisons;
- methods that avoid the imposition of predetermined structures.

These are all issues for establishing the frame of reference within which any statements about a student is to be made. The statement 'John is tall' — if it were the only statement we have about John — could have the effect of conjuring an image of a John whose most striking characteristic is his height; rather than, say, the colour of his hair or the prominence of his nose. It would certainly exclude the possibility of picturing John as short: as does the statement 'John is taller than average', which invites a mental picturing of John in comparison with other people. Saying that he is 'getting taller' invites a comparison between John as he is now and John as he was before. Saying that he is 'fairly tall' establishes a rough-and-ready scale and locates John somewhere above the midpoint — but not so far above it is as 'very tall'. In each case the way the statement is made implies a frame of reference which contains not only this statement but also other possible statements, which *might* — but which are *not* — being made about John. The examples of statements about John given here reduce, to greater or lesser extents, the possibilities of our imagining that John has platinum blond hair, is short, is getting shorter, or is listed in the *Guinness Book of Records* under 'height'.

We might, of course, have been able to say that John is 6 feet 1 inch tall; excluding the possibilities that he is 6 feet 2 inches or taller and that he is 6 feet or shorter. But that kind of measured precision is not available to all aspects of human portrayal. And, even if it were, it would not necessarily be useful to all the needs for which the information is required. And so designing any system of profiling presents difficult problems concerning the establishment of frames of reference. What sort of *possible* statements is the profile going to be capable of conveying? And how is the referencing to make it clear to the user what sorts of statements are being excluded from a particular portrayal?

ACTIVITY

Natural references

Profiling does not have a monopoly on problems for referencing; it is a problem for all the conversations we have (within ourselves and with other people) concerning the people we know. Test this proposition by making ten different statements about yourself. Make them the kind of statements which would be useful on the sort of profile you have it in mind to develop (p.58 provides a quick check list). When you have done it for yourself, make another parallel description of somebody known to you.

Ten statements about me
Ten statements about

What different frames of references appear in your statements about yourself and your statements about other people? Use the following section to analyse the two clusters of statements into the variety of frames of references you use. Can you agree with colleagues about what frames of reference should appear in any profiling system you intend to use?

INPUT

Types of referencing

You may be able to find one or more of the following types of reference in the portrayals you make of yourself and of another person.

Here-and-now self comparisons*: comparing what you are like now in one respect with what you are like now in other respects:

‘I'm more of a talker than a listener.’
‘I get more pleasure from music than from anything else.’

Past-present comparisons comparing what you are like now with what you were like before:

‘The older I get the less I worry!’
‘I can't run upstairs any more . . .’

Statements of potential: comparing what you are like now with how you might be in the future:

‘ . . . but by the spring I am going to get myself fit again.’
‘I want to learn the clarinet’ (this is potential — at least in the sense that wanting to do it makes it significantly more likely that you will do it).
‘I don't want to go pressuring myself like this forever!’ (and not wanting to do it makes it more likely that you'll stop!).

Comparing with others:

‘I am less ambitious than most of my colleagues.’
‘I'm about average in height.’
‘I came 432nd in the London Marathon!’

Comparisons with measures: comparing yourself with a scale:

'I have an IQ of around 135.'
'I'm 5 feet 10 inches tall.'
'I am very co-operative.'

Uncomparative statements: making statements about yourself which appeal to no comparisons:

'I don't like using the telephone.'
'I am fit!'
'I am tall enough to knock a policeman's helmet off !'
'I am methodical in my work.'

---

* There are also 'here-and-there self-comparisons'; but the technical problems they raise are for sources of information, which are considered in the next section.

- The first three types of statement involve comparing self with self: one characteristic with another of the same person's characteristics; how a person is at one time with how he or she is — or might be — at another time. They are *idiographic* assessments. The Greek word *idios* means 'same'.
- The middle two types of statement involve comparison with something outside self — either a group or a measure. The group might be defined (e.g. 'my colleagues'). But it might be implied (e.g. 'average' implies a comparison with people in general). The measure might be regular and apparently precise (most times you can be confident that 5 feet 10 inches means taller than 5 feet $9\frac{1}{2}$ inches, but the difference between an IQ of 135 and 131 is much less reliable). But the measure might be — and often is — implied (e.g. the word 'very' in 'very co-operative' implies a rough-and-ready measure which might contain other points such as 'absolutely co-operative', 'fairly co-operative' and 'not very co-operative'). Where a person is being compared with a group or scale outside him or herself the assessment is said to be *nomothetic*. The Greek word *nomos* refers to the idea of 'standard'.
- The last type is unlike the others, which involve saying that a person has 'more than' or 'less than' of a particular characteristic. These statements *do not appeal to comparisons*, except — perhaps — the comparison involved in saying that a person is 'like this' rather than 'not like this', or 'like this' rather than 'like something else'. They state an independent fact.

EXAMPLES C

Examples of referencing

Examples of profiling techniques with different approaches to referencing are given on the following pages:

- grade referencing;
- norm referencing;
- criterion referencing;
- unreferenced portrayals.

A brief explanation of the main characteristics of each approach is given before each collection of examples.

The table below provides a quick way of identifying which of the formats gives a reasonable chance of gaining what kind of information about students.

Method

Type of reference	Grade referencing (Coded Cg)	Norm referencing (Coded Cn)	Criterion referencing (Coded Cc)	Unreferenced portrayals (Coded Co)
Here-and-now self comparisons	Cg1,2,3,4	Cn3	Cc1,2,3,4	Co1,2
Past-present comparisons	Cg1,2,3,4	Cn3	Cc3	Co2
Potential (present–future comparisons)	Cg3,4	Cn3	Cc1,2,3,4	Co1
Comparisons with others	Cg1,2,3,4	Cn1,2,3		
Comparisons with a measure	Cg1,2,3,4		Cc4	
Uncomparative statements			Cc1,2,3,4	Co1,2

Other examples of various forms of referencing appear elsewhere in the book and are mentioned where appropriate. (P codes refer to Chapter 2, Profiling Profiles, and S codes to Chapter 5, Says Who?)

(Cg) Grade referencing

All the 'Cg' examples are 'counts' or 'measurements' or 'estimates' on scales. They appear to say 'how much' of a quality or characteristic a person has.

The scales commonly contain five or seven points (e.g. A to E, or 1 to 7). Assuming that it is possible or desirable to grade human characteristics, it is rarely plausible, when describing non-physical characteristics, to try to be more accurate than five or seven point scales imply.

All scales have a piece of description at one pole which indicates what the scale is referring to. Examples of one-pole scales are given in Cg1. But some scales are more explicit, carrying descriptions at both ends of the scale — as in Cg2. Some — more explicit still — define each point on the scale, as in Cg3 and 4. But the definitions often invite contributors to do some 'counting', 'measuring' or 'estimating' (however informally and loosely), as evidenced by the frequent appearance of words like 'very', 'usually', 'fairly', 'never', and so on. Sometimes the definitions invite comparisons with other students; examples are words like 'exceptionally', 'normally', 'below average'. Where, as in most of the items given here, the definition of points is done in uncomparative terms the referencing begins to look more like criterion referencing (see section Cc).

Other examples of grade referencing appear in:

P2: First Year Home Base Curriculum Profile (p.15)
P3: Students Personal Progress Record (p.20)
P4: Profile Report and Statement of Achievement (p.24)

Example Cg1: *Graded scale with one pole defined*

SKILLS		1	2	3
First we look at your progress in developing the skills you will need for employment. Each teacher assesses you in some (but not all) areas.	Listening			
Different jobs need a different mix of skills. If you have not developed your skills, fewer jobs may be open to you (especially skilled jobs that need training). This is what your grades mean:	Speaking			
	Reading			
A. You are very skilful in this area, and make good use of your gifts. Good for you.	Writing			
B. You are skilful in this area. This good grade should encourage you.	Remembering			
C. You are fairly skilful, but perhaps you could improve.	Use of diagrams, maps, graphs etc.			
D. Your skill in this area is basic.				
X. Very worrying. Talk over your difficulties with your teachers and family.	Use of number			
	Physical co-ordination			
	Working with your hands			

'Listening', 'speaking', etc. define the scales. The 'A', 'B', 'C' definitions just say 'how much' of the characteristic the student has. There is a teachers' handbook to help assessors to decide which students have which grade. There is room for more than one assessment on each scale.

Source: Strathclyde Department of Education (1979)

Example Cg2:   *Graded scale with both poles defined*

PERSONAL MANNER					
Restless					Placid
Changeable					Consistent
Firm					Flexible
Talkative					Quiet
Impulsive					Thoughtful
Carefree					Anxious

SOCIAL MANNER					
Confident					Shy
Leader					Follower
Co-operative					Unco-operative
Responsive					Reserved
Sociable					Solitary

Source: Anonymous

Example Cg3: *Graded scales with each point defined*

EMPLOYMENT CHARACTERISTICS

Trainee's name .... Date from .... to ....

	A	B	C	D		
TIME KEEPING	Always punctual	Occasionally late	Fairly often late	Regularly late		
ATTENDANCE	Always present	Occasional absence	Days off regularly	Numerous days off		
CONDUCT	Always polite and well-behaved	Usually polite and well-behaved	Generally acceptable, occasional lapses	General conduct not satisfactory		
STANDARD OF WORK	Takes pride in excellent achievement	Good achievement with few errors	Work acceptable but room for improvement	Poor quality work, lacks pride		
ATTITUDE TO WORK	Always keen, interested and industrious	Interested and trying to improve	Accepts all tasks and performs adequately	Lack of interest and enthusiasm		
ATTITUDE TO SAFETY	Totally conscious of safety aspects	Safety conscious for self and tools	Considers safety only when remembers	Very casual in attitude to safety		

OTHER COMMENTS   Supervisor   Trainee comments

Signed .... Supervisor   Signed .... Trainee

Source: Manpower Services Commission (undated, not now available).

Example Cg4: *Graded scales with each point defined*

BEHAVIOUR Consider his/her bearing to those in authority and to his/her contemporaries. Is he/she obliging and pleasant or does he/she co-operate grudgingly?	A	Exceedingly co-operative and helpful.
	B	Pleasant, gets on with others, good general dispositions.
	C	Fairly co-operative.
	D	Unfriendly person — slow to co-operate.
	E	Resentful and unhelpful.
DEPENDABILITY Is he/she trustworthy, reliable and loyal or is he/she totally unreliable?	A	Extremely reliable and adult.
	B	Usually sensible and reliable.
	C	Acts sensibly with occasional guidance.
	D	Acts sensibly under supervision.
	E	Mostly unreliable.
DILIGENCE AND APPLICATION TO WORK Is he/she keen to learn, indifferent or lazy?	A	Exceptionally keen and interested.
	B	Good keen pupil.
	C	Usually interested.
	D	Superficially interested/easily distracted.
	E	Lazy and uninterested.
LEADERSHIP	A	Is usually a leader of groups.
	B	Is a leader when own special skills are required.
	C	Drifts along with the group.
	D	Too easily led.
GENERAL GROOMING	A	Neat and tidy
	B	Sometimes neat and tidy.
	C	Never neat and tidy.
REACTION TO CORRECTION	A	Accepts correction without complaint.
	B	May disagree but will accept punishment.
	C	Is likely to be aggressive and argue.
GENERAL HEALTH	A	Good.
	B	Poor.

Source: Anonymous

(Cn) Norm referencing

Where a grade relies on the manifest use of a process of counting or estimating of occurrence it is relatively easy to read with understanding. But the allocation of some grades on a one-pole scale seems to many a mysterious process of thought. Some assessors might agree that the ascription of 'B' rather than 'C' is as much a matter of intuition as of an accountable process of thought. Normed references use a different basis of account.

All the 'Cn' examples use normed scales which locate the individual student by comparing him or her with a known group. The range is divided into segments, each of which corresponds with a given proportion of the group with which the individual is being compared. The individual is said to be 'near the bottom', 'in the middle', or 'near the top' of that group, rather than being said to have 'a little', 'some', or 'a lot' of a particular characteristic. The frame of reference includes a group with which the individual is being compared.

Often the comparison is with the whole of the student's age group, as in Cn1. This assumes that the assessor will have an accurate-enough impression of how the characteristic is distributed in the age group. Some norm references provide for the closer specification of the group with which the individual is being compared, as in Cn2. Further explanation is sometimes given to the contributors and users of the assessment, by describing the sort of characteristics which are thought typically to occur in each segment on the scale, as in Cn3. Again, where such descriptions can be freed of their comparative connotations, they look more like criterion references (see the next section).

Example Cn1: *General norms scale*

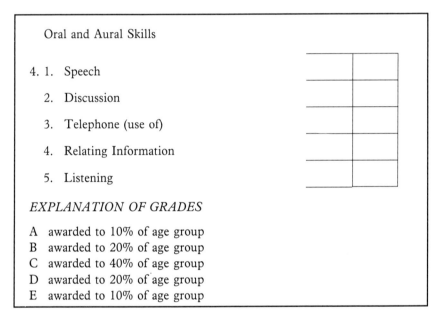

Oral and Aural Skills

4. 1. Speech

   2. Discussion

   3. Telephone (use of)

   4. Relating Information

   5. Listening

EXPLANATION OF GRADES

A awarded to 10% of age group
B awarded to 20% of age group
C awarded to 40% of age group
D awarded to 20% of age group
E awarded to 10% of age group

Source: Balogh, 1982

Example Cn2:   *Specific norms scale* (for a single subject)

ACHIEVEMENT (Tick one) In relation to a normal group of O-level/A-level/CSE/candidates: 16/17/18 year old leavers	
Top 5%	
Above Average	
Median 30%	
Below Average	
Bottom 5%	

ACHIEVEMENT IN RELATION TO ABILITY (Tick one or neither)	
Noticeably above	
Noticeably below	

Source: Anonymous

Example Cn3: *General norms with description on scale*

THE FIVE-FOLD GRADING

	E Grade (10%) very much below average	D Grade (20%) below average	C Grade (40%) average	B Grade (20%) above average	A Grade (10%) very much above average
First Impressions and Physical Makeup	Unkempt and badly dressed. Rough in speech and manner.	Rather scruffy and untidy about details. Slovenly speech and awkward manner.	Reasonably neat and tidy, but undistinguished. Correct speech. Quite at ease on own ground.	Well turned out and carefully dressed. Well spoken with attractive friendly manner.	Perfectly turned out, distinguished appearance; very pleasant voice with charm of manner.
Qualifications and Expectations	Interrupted schooling. No vocational training. Labouring job.	Left school at normal age, but did badly. Some training for a few months. Semi-skilled job.	Left school at normal age, having done well. Apprenticeship. Skilled jobs.	Grammar School to 16–18. Indentured apprenticeship with part-time classes. Supervisory job.	University, professional level of training. Managerial job.
Brains and Abilities	Only able to tackle the very simplest kind of work.	Able to cope with routine work under supervision.	Able to learn work which involves skill and day-to-day planning.	Able to plan the work of others within a framework of policy.	Able to assimilate and interpret detailed information and plan long term developments.
Motivation	Disintegrated personality. Unable to set any goals at all.	Goals either below or unrealistically above capacity. Inconsistent and unpredictable unless carefully supervised.	Sets himself fair goals, and follows them up quite consistently. Could do better.	Goals high in relation to abilities and opportunities. Generally succeeds in what he sets out to do.	Aiming as high as possible, and never deviating from plan. Always achieves grade.
Adjustment	Mental illness. Unable to cope with ordinary life.	Awkward and difficult. Has to have special consideration and careful handling.	Fits in quite well with others, and can take their fair responsibility but with little powers of leadership.	Usually found in significant role. Can take responsibility for others. Doesn't lose his head.	Always found in leadership positions. Takes great responsibility without strain.

(Extract from *Handbook of Employment Interviewing,* by John Munro Fraser)

Source: FEU, 1982

(Cc) Criterion referencing

While grade referencing might be said to offer the same kind of scaled portrayal for a student as a ruler or a strain gauge offers for a piece of string, and norm referencing conveys a notion of length or strength by saying how this compares with other pieces of string, the use of criterion referencing attempts to say what the piece of string is good for. The attempt requires explicit description of what that piece of string — or person — has done, can do or, in some specific respect, is like. Arguments for criterion referencing are closely associated with those for mastery learning. The description may contain some estimation, counting or measuring of occurrence of the 'occasionally', 'usually' or 'frequently' type. But, in principle, comparisons with other students are avoided. The portrayals are of the 'like this' or 'not like this' type; they are not of the 'more than . . .' or 'less than . . .' type.

Criterion references appear on formats that contain a range of descriptions which it might be possible to make of any of the students. The frame of reference is therefore different from that provided by grade and normed referencing. The reader can see what *might* have been said in terms of specific behaviours and characteristics, and can locate in that range of possibilities what *has* — and what has not — been said about this particular student.

Because criterion referencing sets out a range of things it is *possible* to say, it provides the student not only with an account of what has been said but also with an account of what might be said in the future — something to be aimed for. Because criterion referencing is more manifest to the reader than most grade and norm referencing it is also more open to challenge by students.

Criterion referencing sometimes takes the form of simple lists of specific abilities or other characteristics, which the student is assessed as having or not having — as in Cc1. But a problem is that, if the descriptions are to be sufficiently specific to be clear, then the total list will be very long; so profiles can subdivide general criteria into more specific elements which, for the sake of brevity, are numbered — as in Cc2. Sometimes the criteria are arranged in a hierarchy which resembles a scale — as in Cc3. Sometimes criteria are used in association with a scale — as in Cc4.

Other examples of criterion referencing appear in:

P5:   School Leaving Profile (p.28)
P7:   Certificate of Vocational Preparation (p.39)
P8:   Profile Folder (p.45)

Example Cc1: *Criterion referenced portrayal*

This is part of a practical profile scheme designed to be applied to a variety of different courses. It is expected that the scheme will be used in many different subject areas as portrayals of core skills. The scheme comprises: Practical Communiction Skills (part of which is set out below); Practical Numeracy Skills (part of which is set out in example Cc2); and Practical Manual Skills. Final certificates include lists of skills taken from records like this in which the student has demonstrated competence.

SKILLS DEALING WITH PEOPLE — TASK AND DATE						
A1 Establish working relationships with individuals						
A2 Establish working relationships as a member of a group		*The tutor ticks the box in which the student has demonstrated this skill in a particular assignment.*				
A3 Relay given information orally to an individual						
A4 Relay given information orally to a group						
A5 Ask questions in order to gain information for a specific purpose						
A6 Make and carry out arrangements (in accordance with a stated goal)						
A7 Give instructions (in order that a particular task can be completed)						
A8 Take instructions (in order that a particular task can be completed)						
A9 Describe an object, person or event (so that it can be recognised and appreciated)						
A10 Explain a process or sequence of events (so that it can be followed)						
A11 Open, conduct and close a brief transaction (in accordance with a stated purpose)						
A12 Open, conduct and close a brief transaction (in accordance with a stated purpose) by telephone						
A13 Listen to each point of view presented in discussion and when asked re-state it accurately						
A14 State own point of view in a discussion (clearly and appropriately)						

A15 Distinguish fact from opinion during a discussion						
A16 Judge the validity of arguments presented in discussion						
A17 Express disagreement without provoking hostility in discussion						
A18 Participate effectively in the negotiation of a possible course of action						

Source: Royal Society of Arts (undated b)

Example Cc2: *Criterion referenced portrayal*

Skills Task and Date						
M1 Measuring Length						
M2 Measuring Height						
M3 Measuring Capacity						
M4 Measuring Temperature						
M5 Measuring Time						
M6 Measuring Two-Dimensional Shapes						
M7 Measuring Three-Dimensional Shapes						
M8 Sorting						
M9 Sequencing						
M10 Place Value						
M11 Application of Number						
M12 Further Applications of Number						
M13 Calculators						
M14 Maps and Plans						
M15 Graphic Representation						
M16 Mathematical Language						

The tutor uses the box in which the student has demonstrated this skill in general way, but using a specific code — examples of which are shown on p.80

CODES M1–3

M1 LENGTH	M2 WEIGHT

1.1   Estimating/approximating length
1.2   Measuring length
1.3   Using the metric system for length
1.4   Using the imperial system for length
1.5   Converting between metric/imperial
        units of length
	2.1 Estimating/approximating weight
	2.2 Measuring weight
	2.3 Using the metric system for weight
	2.4 Using the imperial system for weight
	2.5 Converting metric/imperial units
	        of weight

M3 CAPACITY	
3.1 Estimating/approximating capacity 3.2 Measuring capacity 3.3 Using the metric system for capacity 3.4 Using the imperial system for capacity 3.5 Converting between metric/imperial units of capacity	

Source: Royal Society of Arts (undated b)

Cc3: *Grid-arranged criteria*

The material which incorporates this grid was trialled in Hertfordshire schools in 1983. The County Council retains copyright.

		Int	Final		Int	Final		Int	Final		Int	Final
Problem recognition	Can describe simple problem in limited fashion			Can clearly state a problem with some analysis			Can clearly state problem and specify most aspects of it			Can precisely define problem and enumerate all aspects of it		
Investigation	Can find information with guidance			Can use standard sources of information			Can assemble information from a variety of sources			Shows initiative in seeking and utilizing information from a wide range of sources		
Problem Solving	Can follow routine procedures with guidance			Can fault-find following standard procedures			Can select alternative solutions to given problems			Can independent-ly derive and implement solution to a variety of problems		
Evaluation	Can assess own work with guidance			Can assess own performance on routine tasks in-dependently			Can assess own performance and identify possible improve-ments			Can assess own work critically, relate problems to original brief, suggest future work		
Reading and Writing	Can understand simple texts and write brief notes and reports			Can follow and give straight-forward descriptions and explanations			Can use instruction manuals etc. and write clear, accurate reports			Can abstract & interpret information from a variety of sources and communicate this effectively		
Talking and Listening	Can understand simple instructions and give messages			Can follow and give straight-forward oral instructions			Can follow and give more complex instructions and speak easily about own work			Adept in most verbal encounters; can explain work to strangers, in groups or individually		

Visual Understanding and Expression	Can interpret simple visual displays such as circuit diagrams		Can produce simple 2D sketches and diagrams		Can give clear explanation using sketches and diagrams		Can communicate complex ideas graphically or with models; good design ability	
Safety	After demonstra- tion can use equipment safely for simple tasks		With guidance can use equipment safely for variety of tasks		Can select and use suitable equipment without help		Can set up and maintain equipment; can remedy faults	
Dexterity and Co-ordination	Can use routine hand tools		Can reliably perform basic manipulative tasks		Can perform complex tasks with reasonable accuracy		Can perform tasks requiring a high degree of control and accuracy	
Working with Peers	Can operate with others when led		Can work with others to achieve common aims		Foresees and understands results of own actions in a group		Active, decisive member of a group, helps and encourages others	
Working with those in Authority	Can follow instructions and perform simple tasks under supervision		Can follow instructions and carry them out in- dependently		Can carry out variety of tasks with minimum instructions		Can carry out tasks independent- ly and communicate well with teachers	

Source: Hertfordshire Education Department

Example Cc4: *Criterion-referenced portrayal associated with a scale of grades*

Profile Statement for a Course in Technician Studies

Unit: Workshop Processes and Materials 1 (U80/681) Value: 1.0

Student:

College:

Date:

Unit General Objectives for the student are that he/she:	Performance*			
	NA	*3*	*2*	*1*
A. *Safety hazards*				
1. Identifies the hazards in a workshop environment.				
2. Knows the appropriate procedure in the event of workshop accidents.				
3. Knows the importance of safe electrical working in protecting life and property.				
4. Knows procedures when persons are in electrical danger.				
B. *Hand and Machine Processes*				
5. Selects hand tools for given tasks.				
6. Performs marking out exercises on plane surfaces such as marking out profiles.				
7. Uses simple measuring equipment.				
8. Carries out basic sheet metal operations.				
9. Produces holes in metals and plastics.				
10. Uses a centre lathe.				
11. Describes the selection and maintenance of cutting tools and the need for cutting fluids.				
12. Describes the uses of shaping machines, milling machines and grinding machines.				
C. *Fastening and Joining*				
13. Recognises various joining methods and their applictions.				
14. Describes the methods used in making electrical connections and makes soldered connections.				
15. Describes the principles involved in silver soldering, welding and brazing.				
D. *Working in Plastics*				
16. Appreciates the techniques available within a conventional workshop for producing shapes in plastic materials.				
E. *Materials*				
17 Knows the general properties and uses of common engineering materials.				
18. Knows the reason for and methods of protecting materials from atmospheric attack.				

*an entry of X in NA means not yet assessed, 3 means the student has been assessed but needs more practice, 2 the student has shown basic competence and 1 the student has shown a high degree of competence.

General Comments:

Signed: Status:

Source: FEU, 1982

(Co) 'Unreferenced' portrayals

The only truly unreferenced profile is written on a blank sheet of paper. As soon as any question or other cue is put on the paper then a frame of reference for what might be put down has been suggested. However, the examples that follow seek to reduce the cueing of portrayal to a minimum. The intention is for the portrayal to be made in a frame of reference chosen by the person making the portrayal. They are largely comprised of short cues, open questions and blank spaces.

It is sometimes argued that such recording is not profiling at all, because of the lack of any pre-structuring and because the intention is to record events and not to report skills or personality. But the examples are not entirely free of structuring; nor of any element of assessment. The differences between such portrayals and narrowly defined profiles are primarily differences in the *degree* of use they make of structuring and assessment.

Co1 is a joint portrayal made by the student and his or her teacher, employing a journal format, and an account of next steps to be taken. Co2 is a portrayal to be made wholly by the student, which might be capable of use in support of an application for a job or a place on a training scheme.

Other examples of 'unreferenced' portrayal formats appear in:

P4:   Profile Report and Statement of Achievement (p.24)

P6:   Record of Achievement (p.33)

Ss13:   Record of Self-Directed Learning (p.118)

Co1: *Jointly maintained record*

This was designed as part of a 'logbook' to be included in the student's folder — for a system or portrayal like that in example P8. Source: FEU, 1982.

RECORD OF EXPERIENCE

Name of student/trainee ....

Name and type of scheme ....

....

Name of tutor(s)/supervisor(s) ....

....

Starting date .... End date ....

Profile completion date ....

College/school ....

(Address) ....

....

....

Company/Organization (if applicable) ....

(Address) ....

....

....

Outline of scheme

Details of work experience and opportunity for developing work-related skills

(i)

DAILY RECORD OF EXPERIENCE   WEEK NO: .... *BEGINNING:* ....

Record what you are doing during the week entering each day the answers to the following questions.

> 1.   What did you do and where?
>
> 2.   Who helped you?
>
> 3.   What did you do that was new?

MONDAY

1.

2.

3.

TUESDAY

1.

2.

3.

WEDNESDAY

1.

2.

3.

THURSDAY

1.

2.

3.

FRIDAY

1.

2.

3.

(ii)

WEEKLY REVIEW   WEEK NO: ....   *BEGINNING:* ....

(TRAINEE)

What did you especially enjoy during the week and why?

Was there anything you did *not* enjoy and if not, why not?

(SUPERVISOR/TUTOR)

What has the trainee done particularly well?

After discussion, we have agreed that progress has been made in:

but attention needs to be paid to:

Signed: ....   Signed: ....
(Trainee)   (Supervisor/Tutor)

Date: ....   Date: ....

(iii)

Source: Further Education Unit, 1982

Co 2:   *Student-maintained record*

The material — published as *Record of Personal Experience* — is designed to enable students to make a record of those events and experiences which they judge are worth recording. It is intended that the accounts will portray something about students' attitudes and values as well as about their interests and abilities. The student is introduced to the use of the materials by stages. Part of the preparation, which can be incorporated into group-work, is to invite students to identify most 'liked' activities and 'best' skills. Supporting notes contain suggestions about the sorts of things students might want to record, and also explain how the materials can be used to make that record. Students are encouraged to make 'factual', 'truthful' and 'interesting' accounts of their experiences. It is required that the experiences recorded will be 'substantial' ones — not transient or random events. After some practice with the use of the materials, with assistance from tutors, students can make as many different records of different experiences as they require. The records are written on cards, stored in a folder which is the student's property. The cards provide for portrayal of such experiences as: the student's membership of groups; his or her use of craft skills; creative activity; journeys and visits; learning experiences; physical activities; service to others; and experience of working with others. The student makes all the entries, without interference; but each entry is signed by someone in a position to know that the particular experience or activity has occurred. Although maintaining the record is designed to be principally an educative experience for the student, students are encouraged to think of taking their folder with them for a job interview.

Indications of the layouts of the cards are given below:

CRAFT

Date   Description of things made

ATTENDANCE

This card records attendance at an activity over a period of at least two months.

Activity _____

Time _____   Place _____

From _____   To _____

Record

Sources: Springline Trust and Stansbury, 1980. [*Please note:* Springline Trust does not provide material for selective use or adaptation. The intention is that participating schools and colleges will adopt the programme and its philosphy, and remain in contact with other users so that further developments can be a matter of joint responsibility with the trust.]

EXPLORATION

Second thoughts on referencing

Grades

Grades quantify assessment; although they do not necessarily use letters or numbers. Sometimes they use words like 'extremely', 'frequently', 'usually', or 'fairly' which require that somebody has — however loosely — done some counting, measuring or estimating. Grade referencing compares a person with a scale. A scale can give the same sort of information as a ruler can give about a piece of string. But whereas most people have a usable idea of what the difference between one inch and two inches is, it is much less easy to be sure about what the difference between 'excellent' and 'good' (or 'A' and 'B') is on a scale. Teachers may feel that they do know the differences between the points on a scale. It is a claim that can easily be put to the test. If they agree with each other in the grades they assign to the same youngsters in a given situation then the scale is, to that extent, reliable (see the introduction to Chapter 2, Profiling Profiles). It would be worth finding out just how reliable such scales are before they are introduced into any format you are developing. (Norm and criterion referencing can be reliability tested in much the same way.)

In order to improve their reliability many graded scales incorporate descriptions at each point on the scale (as in Cg3 and Cg4). Where such descriptions rely on the use of words like 'extremely', 'fairly' and 'little' they are adding very little to the number or letter scale. Where the descriptions are sufficiently descriptive to convey something about what students do and are, then — for some intentions — the attempt to quantify will not be necessary; the descriptions provide enough of a frame of reference by themselves.

Grades can only be important for intentions which require that one aspect of a student is (idiographically) compared with another aspect of the same student, or where one student is to be (nomothetically) compared with others. Scales like those in Cg2 would, at least, make such comparisons possible. But Cg2 has avoided the use of positively loaded descriptions at one end of the scale and negatively loaded descriptors at the other. Example Cg4 has not: and there can be troublesome consequences for such value-laden polarisations (see Chapter 6, Word Perfect?).

Norms

Norms introduce a further frame of reference into the quantification of assessment, by comparing the student with a group. The simplest form of norming is to count where that student comes in relation to the other students being assessed. If the student is rated 80th among 250 students he or she appears at the 32nd percentile (80/250 × 100), and would appear as norm C in examples Cn1 and Cn3, but as 'below average' in example Cn2. Deciding where to draw lines across the percentiles will, in any event, have consequences for how particular students are portrayed.

For such a procedure to have any validity at all the total group needs to be large enough for it to be likely that it is representative of the general population from which it comes. It is extremely doubtful whether that is usually the case, even for some nationwide samples entered for external examinations. Cohorts can vary from year to year — and, if they do, so will the standards (the frame of reference) defined by normative assessments.

It is even less likely that the smaller group of students in a particular school or college will be representative of anybody but themselves. And so few of the norming procedures shown here use the simple method. Instead they invite teachers, not to count, but to make an estimate about where they locate a particular student in relation to a general population, not just those who happen to be in the sample being assessed. This means that the sample in the school can be portrayed as different from the general population — with more near the top, or the bottom, of the scale. It requires, however, that teachers are able to visualise the distribution of that characteristic in the general population.

An argument for norming portrayals is that it corrects the invalidating distortions caused by teachers who habitually mark 'high' (all their geese are swans), or 'low' (all their sheep are goats), or in the middle (they won't discriminate). It requires that the full range of possible assessments is used — so that a few get very 'high', the majority are spread across the middle range, and a few get very 'low' positions on the range, in a 'curve of normal distribution'. That curve is used in examples Cn1, 2 and 3; the proportion of a general population thought to belong to each category is given as a percentage-of-the-population quantification. That procedure, if it works, will also have the effect of standardising portrayals, so that information coming from one school or college can be compared with information coming from another. It would, in that event, be useful to people who need to compare one student with others. But it seems unlikely that all human characteristics can be distributed on a symmetrical curve of normal distribution.

Some normed assessments are accompanied — as they are in example Cn3 — with descriptions of what each part of the population is thought to be like. Where the descriptions are sufficiently descriptive, the norms — for many purposes — would not be necessary. But, in any event, it seems doubtful that a description can be made of a proportion of a population which accurately separates them from other parts of the range. The combination of norming and description is like telling the relative length of a piece of string and what it is good for in one breath. In the case of Cn3 more description might have proved useful in order to say what each of the categories (such as 'brains and abilities') being 'measured' represents.

Criteria

Receiving a grade 'E' on an ill-defined scale can be like being jeered and booed without knowing why — nasty and not particularly illuminating. Receiving a 99th percentile norm is like receiving the biggest round of applause — but still not knowing quite what is being applauded. Where they receive *only* grades and norms students have to guess. Party games have been invented to exploit the fun to be had from manipulating confused victims with rounds of applause on undeclared criteria. What power they give to the audience! Criterion references use descriptions — not normative comparisons — in order to convey information and impression about students. The use of a well-written criterion reference will conjure in the mind a recognisable and specific picture of what this student has done, can do, or is like.

Some criterion referencing arranges descriptions in a hierarchical sequence ranging from 'basic' to 'advanced' levels. Where a number of categories of hierarchically ordered descriptions are arranged side by side (as they are in examples Cc3 and P8) the method is called 'grid-type' profiling. The grid arrangement provides for some degree of idiographic comparison, pointing out where the relative 'strengths' and 'weaknesses' of the individual student lie.

But criterion referencing has its problems. Producing a comprehensible list of descriptions, which can be used with a sample of students at all levels of achievement, and which is sufficiently specific to be recognisable, means generating a very long list of items (as examples Cc1, P7 and P5 illustrate). Where items are to be generated only for one area of the curriculum the problem of bulk is eased — although even in such cases some systems take special measures to deal with the number of criteria (as in the case of Cc2).

In some cases hierarchies are arranged so that they describe only the middle range of abilities; beginning on the left with descriptions of the 'has made a genuine gain' type, and ending on the right before descriptions of exceptional achievement and value come into view. Example P8 uses this technique to reduce the length and increase the precision of its hierarchy of criteria; providing codes to show where students have not yet reached the most basic level and where they have exceeded the most advanced.

Where criteria are arranged hierarchically — and especially where they are arranged in grid format — there is an implication that descriptions at each level in each category are of roughly equal value. There is also an implication that progress through the levels is roughly equally spaced and will occur in the sequence indicated by the levels on the form. Indeed the designers of example P8 specifically reject the possibility of 'box skipping', and envisage evidence of continuous progress through all the stages laid out on the profile.

Students have been reported to resent the trivial content or patronising tone of some of the criteria entered in the left-hand column of some grid-type profiles; the criteria do not, it seems to the students, represent any achievement or quality of any real significance. Producing a list of descriptions which represents something achievable by all students, but will not invoke the scorn of some, is a difficult task. Example P5 uses computer technology to dispense with 'basic' descriptions of 'advanced' students in numerical skills.

Whether grids or lists are used, criteria are notoriously difficult to write. Arriving at a description which unambiguously conjures up a recognisable picture of what a person has done, can do or is like — without appealing to some covert use of comparison — is a demanding task (see Chapter 6, Word Perfect?). There is a reported tendency to impose upon the use of hierarchically arranged criteria a prior assumption about where it is expected a particular student will come, as though the range of criteria represents a scale or a normal distribution. The sharper and more recognisable the description represented by the criteria, the less likelihood they will be confused with grades and norms.

Criteria of the 'has done' type simply say that something has been achieved at least once, and that is all. Criteria of the 'can do' and 'is like' type build an interpretation upon observation — that because the student has 'got it' once, then he or she has 'got it' indefinitely and in all circumstances. Professor Higgins made just such a mistake concerning Eliza Doolittle. There is a now-you-see-me-now-you-don't quality about a great deal of human performance and behaviour. Some criterion referenced portrayals resort to the use of accompanying scales to accommodate this fact (see example Cc4); and half-way hatching grid profiles like that in Sc5 introduce an element of scaling to each category, implying a more 'limited' than 'complete' attribution of the characteristic. Other criteria referenced profiles (like P8) deal with unwanted implications of generalisability by describing the specific situations from which the portrayal has been derived.

Finally, the idea that criterion referencing is comparison-free may yet prove to be more of a hope than a realisation of the technique. It is not at all difficult to imagine, say, employers counting the number and level of criteria used in portrayals like P7 and P8, and using that quantification to compare one student with another. It is wholly arguable that people who want to avoid having students compared with others should forget about public portrayal altogether. Once the portrayal is made people who need to compare one student with another will find a way of doing it. That news may be less than totally disastrous to your ears: but it has a consequence for design. In the interests of equity it requires that the categories and criteria which appear on any profile should not arbitrarily discriminate against students on certain courses, or against students who because of cultural, ethnic or sexual socialisation do not engage in certain kinds of activities. It means writing criteria on a spread of categories which gives every one portrayed the same chance of showing what they can do and are like.

All of this means that setting down criteria which are sufficiently specific to be recognisable yet are not trivial or patronising, which establish consistent levels between categories, which progress through hierarchies in the right order, and which give all students the same chance of showing who they are and what they can do, is not a 'back of an envelope' job. It requires more thought, trialing and consultation with users than it invariably gets.

Chapter 6, Word Perfect?, re-addresses many of the issues raised here — particularly relating to the task of writing descriptions which are sufficiently objective, value neutral, and anchored to the context in which the assessment is made.

Unreferenced portrayal

Making a graded, normed or 'can do' criterion referenced portrayal involves taking evidence into one's head and coming to a judgement about it; by saying where, within a prestructured frame of reference, this particular student should be located. It is to that extent an interpretation of events. But examples Co1, Co2, P4 and Ss13 all invite us to set down events and actions in a raw form. People are invited simply to say what they see, hear, do and feel. No interpretation is asked for. In that sense, they are records of the facts, rather than interpretations of them.

But the distinction between record and interpretation is clearer in the conception than in the reality. The only way to be completely uninterpretive is to say everything that it is possible to say about every event that has occurred. The act of selecting events is interpretive — interpreting what is thought to be more relevant, or interesting, or illuminating, or whatever. Furthermore, most loosely structured documents, casting themselves as 'records' rather than 'profiles', include some cues to contributors concerning the sort of thing that might be put down (P4 is an example). It is a design feature of records like Co2 and Ss13 — in the vanguard of the movement for 'records' rather than 'profiles' — that the student will say something about his or her attitudes and values, interests and abilities and achievements — and these are frames of reference.

Although the difference between more-structured profiles and less-structured records is a matter of degree, it is important. For the examples cited here all leave significantly more opportunity for people to say what they have to say in their own terms. And that means that they can more completely associate the events they record with frames of reference that are significant to them — the contributors.

The educative and formative uses of such approaches to self-portrayal are manifest. Whether they are useful for summative purposes is open to question. But the designers of Co2 and Ss13 claim that the resulting documentation is successfully used by students when they go for interview, and that such documents have proven to be reliably and validly illuminating of student personality.

Some users of summative documents might need to have a more clearly pre-defined frame of reference; so that they know, among all the things that have been said, what it has been decided can *not* be said about this particular student.

Horses for courses

There is no frame of reference that has nothing to offer to some intention for profiling. None is entirely free of problems and difficulties. Some information and impression about students is best handled, for some purposes, in a pre-structured frame of reference. Some information and impression cannot be fitted into pre-arranged frames of reference and should not be so arbitrarily handled. In general, pre-structuring becomes more useful where between-student comparisons are necessary to intentions. They also become more useful where a number of observations need to be collected and collated into a brief and manageable statement. In general, less structured frames of reference become more useful when the intention is to stimulate free and discursive thought and reflection on the part of the contributor — particularly the student. But none of these generalisations is absolute. Some rather tightly structured frames of reference have proved highly stimulating for formative purposes. And some discursive writing has proved useful for summative purposes.

It seems likely that all but the most limited attempts at student portrayal will incorporate a variety of frames of reference; and that the development of such a portrayal should be a matter of consultation, experiment, trial and continuous refinement.

ACTION

Planning the referencing of a portrayal

With some agreement with colleagues concerning intentions, and some idea of the sort of content you agree should be included, it is likely that you can develop or adapt some referencing methods to incorporate into any profiling system you are working on.

A way of doing this would be to take bits of any existing system of recording and reporting, and re-working them so that they use whatever combination of frames of reference you judge to be appropriate, and avoid those that you judge to be inappropriate.

You may prefer to abandon existing systems in your school or college and start again — from scratch or by adapting one of the examples cited here.

It may be helpful to ask:

- Where in the format it is most useful to provide for (idiographic) self-comparisons . . .
  . . . 'this' aspect with 'that' aspect of self?
  . . . past with present?
  . . . present with possible?
- Where in the format it would be most useful to provide for (nomothetic) comparisons external to self . . .
  . . . with other people (and if so which other people)?
  . . . with a scale (and if so with what expectation of reliable grades)?
- Where in the format could descriptive criteria for portrayal be included . . .
  . . . as checklists?
  . . . hierarchically arranged from basic to advanced levels?
  . . . on grids?
- Should some parts of the portrayal contain loosely structured spaces for uncomparative discursive descriptions in contributors' own terms . . .
  . . . with cues as to what might be included?
  . . . with open questions that semi-structure responses?
  . . . with as little interference as possible in what contributors might set down?

In any event it could be useful to ask different sub-groups of colleagues to work on different sorts of material to be incorporated into the portrayal — and then to exhibit the work of each sub-group to the whole — for discussion, comment and refinement.

In task group work in an organisation it is sensible not to go too far with this kind of work until other colleagues and users (including students) have had a chance to look at and comment upon what you are doing.

CHAPTER FIVE

SAYS WHO?

This chapter is designed to help examine:

- methods for getting more than one perspective on a student;
- methods for involving people who are in the best position to make particular parts of a portrayal;
- methods for involving students in self-portrayal;
- methods for getting information and impression from a range of a student's activities.

It is usual for any record or report on a student to have a collection of contributions from more than one source. Profiles and records of achievement also commonly do so — numeracy skills being portrayed by maths teachers, verbal skills by English teachers, and so on. This chapter also considers ways of inviting *different* contributors to talk about the *same* things. Where different contributors are talking about different aspects of the students' life one can speak of a 'collection' of contributions. But where a number of different contributors talk, for example, about verbal skills one can speak of a 'sample' of contributions.

Where sampling occurs one contributor may *confirm* what another says; making it possible to present a portrayal with more confidence. One source may *elaborate* what another says; providing more examples or developing and extending the picture to give it more depth and perspective. One source may *disagree* with another; which can make it difficult simply to portray the student in a few words, but which can also illuminate more of the student's being in more of his or her life. Few human characteristics are devoid of such variabilities.

A central problem for the public or summative use of any widely sampled portrayal is to collate contributions, so that confirmations, elaborations and disagreements are recognised without becoming a source of confusion to users.

Yet, almost all information and impression about a student can be made more reliable by good sampling. And the kind of sample used will make a difference to the kind of portrayal gained.

ACTIVITY

Sampling your life

You can test this for yourself. Ask at least one person who knows you well to write down a list of ten things about you on any *one* ability:

- as a leader;
- as a conversationalist;
- as a sportsperson;
- as a lover;
- in some other 'ability' you decide to portray.

Compare it with your own list of your abilities in.the same area: if you can't do (or won't risk doing) that, imagine what other people who know you well (spouse, colleagues, offspring, students) would say about such a list you have already made for yourself. Do, or would, people who know you well . . .

- say at least one important thing about you which you have not said about yourself?
- dispute any of the statements you have made about yourself?
- make a statement about you which, although similar to your own, has important shifts of emphasis?
- disagree with each other concerning you?

If the answer to any of those questions is 'yes', and if there is no reason to suppose that somebody is seriously deluded, then you have established the case for sampling your own behaviour in order to appreciate the full variety and range of your ability (whichever one it was you all chose to portray).

INPUT

Types of sampling

Differences between the way one person and another see a third can be explained in one or more of the four ways given at the top of the following panel. Opportunities for sampling such variety in a school-, college-, or programme-based profile are given at the bottom.

Coverage for sampling

Time sampling: within the span of a month, or even an hour, people's condition, mood, behaviour and manner change.

Audience sampling: people show different aspects of themselves to different audiences and partners — male and female, family and colleagues, liked and disliked, and so on. Some audiences positively, but often tacitly, invite certain kinds of behaviour; by applauding it — or by provoking it!

Place sampling: circumstances influences behaviour; people do not show the same aspects of themselves at home as at school or college, in formal as in informal settings, in familiar as in unfamiliar places, and so on.

Observer sampling: different observers observe different things. One person will report what another will ignore — usually on the basis of what is significant to him or her.

Opportunities for sampling

School or college in general provide a range of colleagues with an opportunity for observation; in subject work, sports, extra-curricular activity, participation in tutorial time, and so on.

Specifically designed classwork may lend itself particularly to helping teachers and students become more aware of who the students are, what they want, what they are learning, what they want to learn, and so on; preparation and follow-up work in relation to activities such as work experience programmes is often like this.

School-, college-, or programme-sponsored activities (such as work experience placements) may be accompanied by opportunities for students and others to give an account of what the activities illuminate in the student's personality and behaviour.

Other out-of-school or out-of-college activities in which students engage (such as part-time jobs) can also be used as a basis for their own and other people's accounts of who they are and how they are doing.

Face-to-face contact with the students in tutorial, counselling or interview sessions.

EXAMPLES S

Examples of sampling

Examples of existing systems with different methods for sampling are given on the following pages:

- sampling colleagues;
- self-assessments;
- involving people who are not teachers.

A brief explanation of the main characteristics of each method is given before each group of examples.

The analysis below provides a quick way of identifying which of the methods can be used to gain what kinds of sampling, from whom and where.

From whom?

From where?	Colleagues Coded *Sc*	Student self-assessment Coded *Ss*	Other people e.g. peers, acquaintances and employers Coded *So*
From *general school or college activities*	Sc1,2,3,4,5	Ss7,10,12	So1,2
From *specifically designed self-awareness classwork*	Sc4	Ss1,2,3,4,5,11	So1,2,4
From a *sponsored school, college or programme activity*	Sc4,5	Ss1,2,8,9,13	So1,2,3
From *other out-of-school or out-of-college activities*		Ss5,8,11,13	So1,2,3
From *face-to-face contacts* between teacher and student	Sc4	Ss1,2,3,4,6,9 10,13	So1

(Sc) Sampling colleagues

Some aspects of portrayal can be contributed by more than one teacher and, where that is possible, a range of impressions can be gained which will give the resulting portrayal of that aspect more depth and perspective.

Some layouts, such as those in Sc1 and 2, can give a complex and differentiated picture of a student's performance across a range of situations. But there are obvious dangers in circulating such a form to colleagues. There is a well-documented tendency for people to agree with what they can see or hear other people have already said — even if agreeing involves denying the evidence of their own senses. And so it is usual to ask colleagues to make independent assessments on separate slips, like that in Sc3, and to collate the assessments onto a sheet like Sc1 or 2.

But, unlike Sc1 and Sc2, in Sc3 several teachers' assessments are being collated into a single grade. This means that a range of assessments has to be compacted into one. Some systems suggest that the highest grade is taken, few favour simple mathematical averaging. But any process of grading-up or averaging denies part of the purpose of sampling, which is to get as diverse a range of information as possible in order to show human variability.

Other examples also address separate sheets or slips for independent portrayal, as in Sc4 and 5. But Sc5 incorporates a method of collation which is simple and yet retains the diversity of its sample.

Other examples of methods for sampling colleagues appear elsewhere in this book:

P5:   School Leaving Profile (p.28)
P7:   Certificate of Vocational Preparation (p.39)
P8:   Profile Folder (p.45)
Cc1:   Criterion referenced portrayal (p.77)
Co1:   Jointly maintained record (p.85)

Example Sc1 and 2:   *Sampling colleagues on cross-curriculum criteria*

Perseverance																	
Initiative					*Students are rated on a*												
Carefulness					*'below average' to 'well*												
					above average' loosely												
Interest					*normed five-point scale.*												
Reliability																	
Confidence																	
Social competence																	
Leadership																	

Source: ILEA (1982)

Practical and Creative Skills	Art	Agric.	Craft	H.Econ	Music	N.Work	Tec.St	Typing	
1. Has ability in practical work.									
2. Can put theory into practice.									
3. Can work carefully and has a good standard of finish									
4. Is able to evaluate a problem and take steps to solve it.									
5. Can produce original work.			*These are criterion references which are ticked by teachers who observe them.*						
6. Has good co-ordination of hand and eye.									
7. Has appreciation of aesthetic values.									
8. Can use machinery and tools according to safety regulations.									
9. Can use basic tools and equipment competently.									
10. Can read working drawings accurately.									
11. Understands the basic elements of agriculture.									
12. Is able to perform on a musical instrument.									
13. Has a knowledge of the rudiments of music.									
14. Helpful and more.									

Source: Balogh (1982)

Example Sc3:   *Pupil profile where a sample of grades are collated to a single assessment*

S C R E PROFILE
ASSESSMENT SYSTEM

PUPIL PROFILE
Comments

PUPIL'S NAME

Slips like this are circulated to staff for grading. SCRE provides a **Teachers' Guide for the Assessment of Basic Skills** *which defines criteria for each of 4 levels in each skill. The slips can be mounted, overlapped on a peg board, so that each independent assessment can be read side by side by the collating tutor. The tutor is advised to assign 'due weight' to contributing teachers — on the basis of his or her judgement, and their opportunity to assess.*

CLASS GROUP

SKILLS

| LISTENING |
| SPEAKING |
| READING |
| WRITING |
| VISUAL UNDERSTANDING AND EXPRESSION |
| USE OF NUMBER |
| PHYSICAL CO-ORDINATION |
| MANUAL DEXTERITY |

The collated grade is then entered as a tick in the corresponding box in each of these 8 basic cross-curriculum skills. This is one of four pages in a 'School Leaving Report'. Other parts of the system portray 'subject/activity assessment' and 'other observations'.

LISTENING

Acts independently and intelligently on complex verbal instructions ☐

Can interpret and act on most complex instructions ☐

Can interpret and act on straightforward instructions ☐

Can carry out simple instructions with supervision ☐

SPEAKING

Can debate a point of view ☐

Can make a clear and accurate oral report ☐

Can describe events orally ☐

Can communicate adequately at conversation level ☐

READING

Understands all appropriate written material ☐

Understands the content and implications of most writing if simply expressed ☐

Understands uncomplicated ideas expressed in simple language ☐

Can read most everyday information such as notices or simple instructions ☐

WRITING

Can argue a point of view in writing ☐

Can write a clear and accurate report ☐

Can write a simple account or letter ☐

Can write simple messages and instructions ☐

VISUAL UNDERSTANDING AND EXPRESSION

Can communicate complex visual concepts readily and appropriately ☐

Can give a clear explanation by sketches and diagrams ☐

Can interpret a variety of visual displays such as graphs or train timetables ☐

Can interpret single visual displays such as roadsigns or outline maps ☐

USE OF NUMBER

Quick and accurate in complicated or unfamiliar calculations ☐

Can do familiar or straightforward calculations, more slowly if complex ☐

Can handle routine calculations with practice ☐

Can do simple whole number calculations such as giving change ☐

PHYSICAL CO-ORDINATION

A natural flair for complex tasks ☐

Mastery of a wide variety of movements ☐

Can perform satisfactorily most everyday movements ☐

Can perform single physical skills such as lifting or climbing ☐

MANUAL DEXTERITY

Has fine control of complex tools and equipment ☐

Satisfactory use of most tools and equipment ☐

Can achieve simple tasks such as wiring a plug ☐

Can use simple tools, instruments and machines such as a screwdriver or typewriter ☐

Source: Scottish Council for Research in Education (1977) and Broadfoot (1980).

Example Sc4: *'Single-slip' portrayal containing cross-curriculum criteria*

Examples of basic abilities demonstrated in vocationally oriented studies
Vocational Option: Practical Maintenance

1. Working with colleagues 2. Working with those in authority 3. Self-awareness	SOCIAL ABILITIES
4. Talking and listening 5. Reading and writing 6. Visual understanding	COMMUNICATION
7. Using equipment 8. Dexterity and coordination 9. Measuring 10. Calculating	PRACTICAL & NUMERICAL ABILITIES
11. Planning 12. Information seeking 13. Coping with problems 14. Evaluating results	DECISION-MAKING ABILITIES

Such independent portrayals by individual teachers are designed to be used in conjunction with systems like that described in detail as example P8.

Example Sc5:   Grid-type profile and histogram

TRANSFERABLE TECHNOLOGICAL SKILLS

	1 (Basic Level)	2	3	4 — 5 (High Level)
MOTIVATION	Works steadily on most tasks set, but needs guidance and supervision.	Will try again if first attempts do not succeed. Shows interest and willingness in task set.	Determined to be successful and to improve performance even in face of difficulty and if dislikes task.	Will work with enthusiasm on defined task. Determined to be the best.
SOCIAL QUALITIES	Co-operates with others when led. Can be relied on to complete simple tasks if given clear instruction.	Works with others to achieve common aims. Co-operates by responding to instructions, works in an independent manner.	Works effectively when given the minimum of instructions. Reliable member of a team. Recognises personal strengths and weaknesses.	Communicates with those in authority. Can lead others. Inspires confidence. Responds to needs of others.
RATIONAL THINKING AND REASONING	Consider simple problems. Understand clear instructions. Can consider what action to take in simple situations.	Express an argument in logical steps. Form a sensible conclusion. Can exercise some judgement.	Justify actions. Form conclusions by considering all the available evidence. Make sensible decisions.	Can see the consequence of actions. Reject unreasonable views. Make clear, sensible decisions and offer logical argument.
ADAPTABILITY AND FLEXIBILITY	Adapts to new situations if given help and guidance.	Can adapt to changing work conditions and modify ideas.	Is willing to change strategies. Can utilise existing skills in new environment.	Adapt to and promote changing conditions. Can manage uncertainty and work under pressure.
INITIATIVE INDEPENDENCE RESOURCEFUL-NESS	Can work alone for short periods if given clear instructions and supervision.	Can work alone without supervision using the available resources.	Can take initiative. Work independently. Will make full use of available resources and improvise as necessary.	Can take the lead. Can originate new ideas and decide on suitable action. Can use practical ingenuity.
ATTITUDES	Willing to try. Is tidy and orderly.	Appreciates need for accuracy and care. Interested in work. Works safely.	Will persevere in face of difficulty. Efficient and conscientious.	Capable of taking responsibility, open minded and committed. Appreciates quality and excellence.
DISCIPLINE SELF-DISCIPLINE SELF-ORGANISA-TION	Accepts orders and instructions. Works under supervision.	Accepts supervision and control. Recognises need for order, control and training. Punctual.	Can organise own work. Exercises control over personal actions.	Can organise others. Dedicated, efficient and good influence on others.

// indicates completion of first column up to level 1

(i)

The profile identifies cross-curriculum 'qualities', and various versions will be independently completed by teachers; their assessments being collated as asterisks on the histogram on page (ii) of this example.

continued.....

PUPIL PROFILE — PERSONAL QUALITIES

Personal Quality	Basic Level				High Level	
	0	1	2	3	4	5
MOTIVATION	≠	*****	*****	*****	*	
SOCIAL QUALITIES	≠	*****	**			
RATIONAL THINKING AND REASONING	≠	*****	*****	*		
ADAPTABILITY AND FLEXIBILITY	≠	*****	*****			
INITIATIVE INDEPENDENCE RESOURCEFULNESS	≠	*****	***			
ATTITUDE	≠	*****	**			
DISCIPLINE SELF-DISCIPLINE SELF-ORGANISATION	≠	*****	*****	*		

School ....

Pupil's Name ....

Pupil's Age ....

Date ....

{ *Employers may then wish to draw up a transparent template to match against pupil profiles. The template should be determined by the entry level and training requirement of the individual firm. The template is indicated thus* _ _ _ _ }

(ii)

Source: School Technology Forum (1984)

(Ss) Self-portrayal

Students may not expect to be asked to assess themselves or to contribute to their own record. Yet there are some things about themselves that only they know. And, it can be argued, the root of all knowledge is knowledge of self; so self-portrayal may be among the more important of educational experiences.

Some of the examples given here are intended to invite students into a review of where they are, and where they want to be, before they embark upon a new experience; such as beginning a new programme — Ss1 and 2, or going to an interview — Ss3. Some invite self-assessment of aspects of personality in a way which is intended to be of use to students at decision points in their lives — Ss4 and 5. One example is specifically designed to be used with face-to-face help — Ss6. Others are designed to provide a basis for portraying learning as it occurs — Ss7, 8 and 9. Yet others invite students to review a completed phase in their learning — Ss10, 11 and 12. One example is designed to include all of these features in a single programme of self-portrayal activity — Ss13.

In almost all cases the production of a document portraying information and impressions about the student is a secondary or side effect. The main purpose is to offer students the chance to distil and articulate their objectives for learning, to reflect upon how those objectives are best to be realised, to monitor progress, to portray outcomes, and to decide what the best next step might therefore be. The learning experiences referred to are varied: they include the use of classrooms, work experience placements and projects, but also include activities such as thinking about preferred work, going for an interview and leisure-time pursuits. And 'curriculum' for this learning is, therefore, broadly defined. But much of what is set out here is material developed to support 'negotiated curriculum'; that is, curriculum for the content of which the students take their own measure of responsibility.

Other examples of self-portrayal methods appear in:

P4:   Profile Report and Statement of Achievement (p.24)
P5:   School Leaving Profile (p.28)
P6:   Record of Achievement (p.33)
P8:   Profile Folder (p.45)
Co1: Jointly Maintained Record (p.85)
Co2: Student Maintained Record (p.88)

Example Ss1: *Preparatory self-reviewing — checklist*

TRAINEE SELF REVIEW: GOALS (OBJECTIVES)

Which of the following would you say are reasons why you came to (name of organisation) or are goals (objectives) which you would like to achieve while on the scheme.

Personal

To get to know myself better.
To like myself more.
To become more confident.
To become more self-disciplined.
To know more about what I want to do with my life.
To get better at making decisions.
To become more adaptable and mobile.
To get better at reading and writing.
To become better with numbers.
To manage my money better.
To learn how to manage a home.
To learn more about personal health and hygiene, contraception etc.
To get on better with other people.
To understand other people more.
To communicate with others more.
To trust others more.
To make new friends.

Work

To get to know the sort of job I would like.
To know the sort of job that would suit me.
To want to get a job more.
I want to go to work more.
To enjoy work more.
To get on better with the people whom I work with.
To work better with teams or groups of people.
To know where I can find out about jobs available.

To learn how to write letters of application.
To learn how to fill in application forms.
To become better in interviews.
To become safer at work.
To learn special skills in shop work or warehouse work.

Leisure

To know the range of spare time activities open to me.
To know where these can be done, how much they would cost me.
To know about possible holiday opportunities.
To know how to arrange holidays.
To make better use of my leisure time.
To make better use of my holidays.
To get better at bottle collecting and work at the YMCA also to get better at walking.
To try harder at work even when I collect old bottles.

Other issues

To know more about:
Law and the Police.
Rights and responsibilities.
Race relations.
Politics and government.
Current affairs.
How companies work.
Public and private industry.
Trade unions.
Rights at work.

Is there anything else you would like to learn about while you are a trainee?

Source: Pearce *et al.* (1981b)

Example Ss2: *Preparatory self-reviewing — questionnaire*

TRAINEE INDUCTION FORM

These questions are to help you think about the experiences you have had in the past and the Work Experience Scheme which you are now starting.

You will have an opportunity to discuss your answers with a number of staff.

What full or part-time (paid or unpaid) work have I done in the past? (e.g. paper round)

....

How might this help me now and in the future? ....

How can other experiences at school or at home help me now? ....

What do I expect to gain from this experience? ....

What would I like to get from this experience? ....

What can I do to help myself? ....

What can other people do to help me? ....

What worries do I have about this Work Experience Scheme? ....

Source: Pearce *et al.* (1981b)

Example Ss3: *Checklist of career problems*

Published as The Career Problem Checklist the material is a four-page printed folder, principally a checklist. It is designed to help careers specialists identify students' problems, and as a source of reflection for use by students. The last page is given to more open questions concerning 'other problems' and what sort of help the student is asking for. The number of items checked can be compared with response rates for 'average' groups of students — as a rough-and-ready guide to degree of pressure being experienced. An accompanying teachers' handbook contains suggestions for individual and group use with students. In groups, for example, students can be invited to compare with other members of the group the way they have responded to the items (this can be done without disclosing to other students which particular items have been checked). The checklist can also be used by teachers as a basis for making decisions about curriculum changes. The handbook contains a computer program for collating the findings of the checklist from a group of students. An impression of the content of the checklist is set out below.

Source: Crowley 1983

Name ....
Age ....
Date ....
School/College ....
Type of course ....

This check list has been prepared to help you indicate the kinds of problems you may be having in planning your career.
By using the information given here, the careers teacher or careers officer will be in a better position to help you with your career plans

INSTRUCTIONS
Inside this folder is a list of problems often faced by school or college leavers
Read through the list carefully and if you see an item which describes the way you feel at the moment, underline it

For example: **I am having problems:**
14   in finding out about local jobs

When you have completed the list, go back over the items you have underlined and put a circle around the numbers of any items which are particularly important to you.

For example: **I find that:**
㉕ I am unable to make decisions

AT SCHOOL OR COLLEGE
I am having problems:

1   in choosing the rights subjects
2   in studying certain subjects
3   in coping with teachers
4   in worrying about exams
5   by missing work through illness
6   through taking subjects I don't like
7   through getting poor reports
8   in giving choice of job any serious thought
9   in using the careers room
10   in discovering my job interests
11   in discovering my abilities
12   in discovering what kind of a person I am
13   in finding out about jobs in general
14   in finding out about local jobs
15   in finding out about college courses
16   in applying for college courses
17   in getting information on grants
18   in getting some useful work experience
19   in finding someone who can give me advice

DECISIONS
I find that:

20   I don't know when to leave school/college
21   I may have to leave earlier than I want to
22   I want to leave but am not allowed to
23   I can't work out what I want to do
24   I keep changing my mind about jobs/courses
25   I am unable to make decisions
26   other people are making decisions for me
27   I am under pressure to conform

AT HOME
I have problems:

28   through my health or a handicap
29   studying at home
30   talking to my parents/guardians
31   in getting others to agree with my plans
32   in not being allowed out very much
33   through my parents/guardians expecting too much of me
34   in finding a part-time or holiday job
35   in finding somewhere to live
36   in not having enough money

A PARTICULAR JOB
I have a job in mind but don't know enough about:

37   entry qualifications required
38   methods of entry
39   methods of training
40   duties involved
41   people I'll have to work with
42   effects of the job on my life
43   interests required
44   abilities or skills required
45   whether I'm the right kind of person
46   chances of my getting the job
47   wages and rewards
48   hours of work
49   working-conditions
50   prospects for the future

Example Ss4: *Self-inventory of successes and failures*

	Not a problem for me	I can succeed if I try	I usually fail
1. Wanting a job			
2. Applying for jobs			
3. Being interviewed			
4. Settling in			
5. Getting on with workmates			
6. Getting on with supervisors			
7. Timekeeping			
8. Getting my rights			
9. Staying in jobs			
10. Developing skills			

Source: Scottish Vocational Preparation Unit 1982

Example Ss5: *Self-assessment of values and needs*

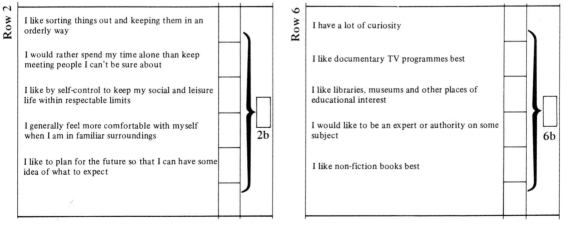

Row 2

I like sorting things out and keeping them in an orderly way

I would rather spend my time alone than keep meeting people I can't be sure about

I like by self-control to keep my social and leisure life within respectable limits

I generally feel more comfortable with myself when I am in familiar surroundings

I like to plan for the future so that I can have some idea of what to expect

2b

Row 6

I have a lot of curiosity

I like documentary TV programmes best

I like libraries, museums and other places of educational interest

I would like to be an expert or authority on some subject

I like non-fiction books best

6b

The checklist in Ss5 is arranged in columns and rows. The columns refer to perceptions of self: at school or college; in out-of-school or -college pursuits; and in personal opinions on social issues. These examples come from the column referring to out-of-school or -college pursuits. The rows correspond to the eight types of motive set out in the input section in the chapter on 'Telling What?'. These examples refer to motives for 'security' and 'curiosity'. Each student ticks the statements which apply to him or her, double or treble ticking any that more especially seem to apply. The whole checklist can be scored for each of the eight types of motive. The scores are crude and provide only for self-comparisons. But they are used in the original material as a basis for searching for alternative future possibilities which promise to offer the sort of satisfactions sought by the student. Suggestions for classroom use are included in a teachers' manual.

Source: Law 1977

Example Ss6: *Card sorts*

'I can do these now'

'These I need help with'

CAN YOU EXPLAIN THINGS TO PEOPLE ?

Example: How to get to the local bus station.

Example: The rules of a game such as monopoly, football, netball, etc.

13

CAN YOU FOLLOW VERBAL INSTRUCTIONS ?

Example: Carry out instructions from teacher for the next task etc.

Example: Understand street directions if you have to ask your way in a strange place.

14

CAN YOU WRITE MESSAGES AND NOTES ?

Example: Take down a telephone message for someone.

Example: Make notes during a lesson at school.

Example: Leave a note for your mum if you go out.

16

CAN YOU USE EVERYDAY TOOLS ?

Examples: Scissors

Hammer.

Hand-Whisk.

Paintbrush.

Screwdriver.

Etc.

18

CAN YOU USE PUBLIC TRANSPORT SUCH AS A BUS OR A TRAIN ?

Example: Plan and make a coach journey from your home town to London.

Example: Organise a journey by train to watch an away game by a local football team.

19

CAN YOU USE A PUBLIC OR PRIVATE TELEPHONE ?

Example: To obtain an ambulance if there was an accident in the street.

Example: To telephone for a taxi to pick you up at your home.

21

CAN YOU READ A DIAGRAM OR A MAP ?

Example: Read a local street map.

Example: Follow a diagram on how to fit an electric plug.

11

CAN YOU TALK TO PEOPLE YOU DON'T KNOW VERY WELL ?

Example: Careers Officers.

Employers.

Supervisor.

College Staff.

Etc.

12

CAN YOU FOLLOW WRITTEN INSTRUCTIONS ?

Example: Follow instructions on a cake mix packet.

Example: Follow assembly and fitting instructions on a model kit.

Example: Filling in a form.

15

CAN YOU WRITE A LETTER TO GET OR TO GIVE INFORMATION ?

Example: Write to a company to ask if they have any job vacancies.

Example: Write to a friend to arrange a meeting.

17

CAN YOU USE A REFERENCE BOOK, MANUAL, OR A DICTIONARY IN ORDER TO FIND INFORMATION ?

Example: Find the address of a local plumber from the Yellow Pages.

Example: Look up a word in a dictionary.

20

Students are given cards to read and are asked to put them into two piles.

Source: Corby Careers Office, 1982. (Developed by Northamptonshire County Council in conjunction with the Manpower Services Commission)

Example Ss7:   *Self-assessment in a school or college subject*

This is part of a document addressed to anyone who would take an interest in a conventional school report. It is produced by teacher and student each half-term, portraying achievement in English Studies. It includes an explanation of its purpose; and a description of the course content and skills involved in the course. The remainder of the four-page A4 card-covered document is set out below.

Written work to date	Comment
Completed by student	

There is more space for writing on the original.

SKILLS — GRADES		1 = I find this difficult 5 = I feel I am competent in this	
Expressing ideas on page		Editing writing to improve it	
Choosing the right words to do so		Recognising irrelevant passages	
Using punctuation correctly		Proof-reading for mistakes	
Spelling acurately		Note taking of important points	
Explaining ideas to others		Using notes when writing essays	
Describing things in words		Writing imaginative pieces	
Listening attentively to others		Writing about books, plays, poems	
Listening to a story or poem		Discussing/listening to other views	
Reading with attention to detail		Expressing personal views in a group	
Preparing for essay writing by reading a text carefully and selecting the useful episodes		Reading books for pleasure	
ADD ANY EXTRA SKILLS HERE ...		Submitting work on time	

```
┌─────────────────────────────────────────────────┐
│                 ACHIEVEMENTS                     │
├─────────────────────────────────────────────────┤
│         ...................................... student │
└─────────────────────────────────────────────────┘
```

```
┌─────────────────────────────────────────────────┐
│                 ACHIEVEMENTS                     │
├─────────────────────────────────────────────────┤
│         ...................................... staff │
└─────────────────────────────────────────────────┘
```

```
┌─────────────────────────────────────────────────┐
│  the next step ...                               │
│                                                  │
│         (This is written by the student)         │
│                                                  │
└─────────────────────────────────────────────────┘
```

(ii)

Source: Ernulf Community School

Example Ss8: *Timesheet*

TIMESHEET		TASK OR PRODUCT	MATERIALS INVOLVED	SKILLS AND TECHNIQUES INVOLVED	TIME TAKEN (HOURS)	GENERAL COMMENTS WEEK NO
DAY						
MONDAY	AM					
	PM					
TUESDAY	AM					
	PM					
WEDNESDAY	AM					
	PM					
THURSDAY	AM					
	PM					
FRIDAY	AM					
	PM					

Source: Pearce, *et al.* (1981b)

Example Ss9:   *Report of experience — 'stems'*

I came to (name of programme) because . . .

I chose this placement/project because . . .

My job is . . .

I am responsible to . . .

The things I like most about this opportunity are . . .

The things I like least about this opportunity are . . .

I work with . . .

The courses I have completed at (name of programme) are . . .

The thing I like/dislike most about these courses . . .

The things that will help me get a job are . . .

I have been considering these job vacancies . . .

Places I look for these jobs are . . .

I have the following problems . . .

My suggestions for improving (name of programme) are . . .

The original leaves room for the student's responses to each sentence 'stem'.

Source: Pearce, *et al.* (1981a)

Example Ss10:   *Retrospective self-reviewing questionnaire*

The following reviews are included for repeated use in a ring-binder to be maintained by students on a training scheme. The student is invited to maintain a daily record of experience, undertake periodic reviews, and discuss with his or her tutor the learning which is coming from its use. The total document, which can run to more than a hundred pages over the course of a year-long scheme, also contains a record of key contacts on the scheme; of skills assessed at induction; of notes made on particular pieces of work undertaken; of notes made by the tutor — after each review session — on how the learning is developing and what action has been agreed to consolidate strengths and improve weaknesses; an occasional profiling of employment characteristics and portrayal of work skills attained; a list of work placements to which the student has been assigned; and a final grid-type profile agreed by the student and tutor at the end of the scheme.

RESIDENTIAL EXPERIENCE — TRAINEE REVIEW

If you take part in a residential course as part of your scheme please record each day what you have done by answering the following questions:

1. What have you done today?

2. What did you like the most?

3. What did you like the least?

Each of these panels occupies an A4 sheet in the original, giving room for student responses.

4. How do you think what you have done might help you at work, if at all?

Signed .... trainee

(i)

WEEKLY/DAILY RECORD

Week number ....

1. What new jobs have you done this week?

2. What new skills have you learned?

3. How did you learn these?

4. What did you find easiest to do and why?

5. What did you find hardest to do and why?

6. What tools, equipment, machinery have you used this week?

(ii)

PERIODIC REVIEW — COMPLETE EVERY .... WEEKS

Complete every four/six/eight weeks
of Work Experience and Training

TRAINEE

Record here your views on the scheme so far by answering the following questions:

1. What have you enjoyed the most about the scheme so far?

2. What do you like the least?

3. Have you learnt to do things that you could not do before starting the scheme? Please give examples.

4. What do you think could be done to improve the scheme?

Signed ....   Trainee

(iii)

Source: Manpower Services Commission (undated a, not now available).

Note. The system has been replaced by a simpler version incorporating fewer questions on a weekly and periodic review basis only — see Manpower Services Commission (undated b).

Example Ss11:   *Self-appraisal 'stems'*

A self-appraisal page is included in a document, much of which is given to teachers' accounts of the curriculum and students' performance in it.

The self-appraisal appears on an A4 sheet with the following incomplete sentence 'stems':

- I think I am . . .
- In 5 years' time I think I will be . . .
- Successes during my life . . .
- Disappointments during my life . . .
- Jobs which I have done; e.g. work experience, part-time jobs and work in the community . . .
- Skills I have mastered . . .
- Equipment I have used . . .
- An example of when I was a responsible person . . .
- How I spend my free time . . .
- People who will give me a reference . . .

Source: Norton Priory School

Example Ss12: *Self-appraisal checklist*

This is a draft version of material for inclusion in an eight-page A5 format school-leaving assessment. It was developed to this stage — under severe time constraints — as part of a development project in which the school participated. Other parts of the assessment include room for descriptions of participation in such activities as voluntary work or part-time jobs; in sports and cultural activities; and for the listing of subjects taken, with examination results. Personal qualities and work skills are profiled on scales like those shown below for some of the work skills. Students entries are validated, where possible, by teachers.

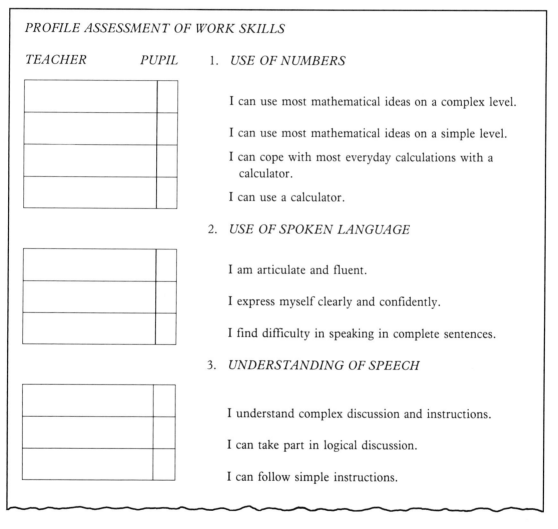

PROFILE ASSESSMENT OF WORK SKILLS

TEACHER   PUPIL   1. USE OF NUMBERS

I can use most mathematical ideas on a complex level.

I can use most mathematical ideas on a simple level.

I can cope with most everyday calculations with a calculator.

I can use a calculator.

2. USE OF SPOKEN LANGUAGE

I am articulate and fluent.

I express myself clearly and confidently.

I find difficulty in speaking in complete sentences.

3. UNDERSTANDING OF SPEECH

I understand complex discussion and instructions.

I can take part in logical discussion.

I can follow simple instructions.

Source: Goacher 1983

Example Ss13: *Record of Self-Directed Learning*

The material — published as the Diamond Challenge Programme — leads to the formation of a record of independent initiative and enterprise. The primary objective of the material is, however, to help students develop their motivation, personal qualities and employability. It is intended for students who are ready to accept responsibility for making a formal contract to carry through to completion activities such as the following: develop a skill; develop an interest; undertake an enquiry or interview; provide a service; complete a teaching and learning programme; or participate in an event, journey or visit. The student accepts the whole responsibility for carrying through the work; teachers help when asked. Students are not protected from natural blocks or people's vetoes on their activities. Each separate contract has a completion date assigned to it by the student, which is not re-negotiable — although elements of one contract can be transferred to a new contract. Students can begin planning the next activity before the present contract is up. Students are taken through the programmes by stages, beginning with a basic group of three activities. But the final record may contain portrayals of between six and twelve activities.

Each activity is carried through in four stages: planning, writing up, reviewing and recording. The recording or portrayal of each activity and its outcomes is set out on an A4 sheet, containing the panels indicated below. The collected record is bound in a plastic covered binder.

Plan

This represents the initial agreement with the teacher concerning the activity. It is articulated to the question 'What do you want to happen?'

Signed
dated

Outcome

These sections are completed at the end of the contract. They are articulated to the questions 'What did happen?' 'Why?' 'What, if anything, was good or memorable or important about it?'

Review

Signed
date

A final summary of activities appears at the end of the binder, authenticated by a teacher.

Source: Springline Trust [*Please note:* Springline Trust does not provide material for selective use or adaptation. The intention is that participating schools and colleges will adopt the programme and its philosophy, and remain in contact with the other users so that further developments can be a matter of joint responsibility with the trust.]

(So) Other people

People other than teachers know students. Those other people include family, peer group, neighbourhood acquaintances, people met in part-time jobs, in social and leisure 'life, and so on. Such contacts offer feedback to young men and women on many aspects of their achievements, capacities and behaviours; in some respects they are better placed to offer such feedback than are teachers in schools and colleges. It is therefore curious that materials designed to help students make use of out-of-school and out-of-college experience — such as work experience programmes — have paid so little attention to inviting students to review what they learn about themselves as individuals from direct and personal contact with the people they meet on such experiences.

Almost all of the material reproduced in this handbook incorporate enquiries addressed to teachers which could be adapted to be addressed to other people; and, in many cases, would receive more useful and more authoritative answers. This section contains examples which have been specifically designed to address such other people. The checklist — So1 — is designed in a way which lends itself to use by a wide variety of people in a variety of settings. Classroom material — So2 — has been developed specifically to invite students to search for feedback on themselves among a variety of acquaintances. Material — So3 — has been developed for recording feedback from voluntary work or work experience placements. And strategies — So4 — have also been developed for use in classrooms inviting students to see their peer groups as sources of feedback. All of these examples represent an aspect of portrayal in which there is still a great deal of room for further development.

Example So1:   *Wide-sampling checklist*

An element of scaling can be introduced to check lists by inviting single-, double- and treble-underlining to indicate degree of agreement.

I   PERSONAL ATTRIBUTES

Persevering   Meticulous   Trustworthy   Inattentive   Tense
   Anxious   Unreliable   Ambitious   Responsible
Fluent   Relaxed   Sensitive   Adaptable   Thorough
   Timid   Irresponsible   Conventional   Impulsive
Inflexible   Careless   Conscientious   Untrustworthy   Reliable
   Self-reliant   Changeable   Easily distracted   Unconventional

II   SOCIAL RELATIONSHIPS

Popular   Persuasive   Polite   Quiet   Co-operative   Dominant
   Aggressive   Unsociable   Solitary   Confident   Self-sufficient
Assertive   Unco-operative   Talkative   Shy   Malleable   Sociable
   Stubborn   Argumentative   Reserved

III   WORKING RELATIONSHIPS

Amenable   Helpful   Isolated   Seeks limelight   Responsive
   Individualistic   Avoids limelight   Follower   Original   Takes initiative
Leader   Leaves tasks uncompleted   Servile   Dictatorial   Team-worker
   Independent   Values   Supervision   Unco-operative

IV   RESPONSE TO PRESSURE

Stubborn   Excitable   Easily discouraged   Unpredictable   Fearful
   Insensitive   Uninterested   Resilient   Unexcitable
Yielding   Calm   Resistant   Stolid   Persistent   Anxious

The original has a blank space for further comment. Although many of the words in this version present problems (see chapter Word Perfect?) the format lends itself to use by a wide range of sources, both inside and outside the school or college. The original is part of a folder containing a range of portrayals of different aspects of the student's life and work. It is used as material for an interview with students. The format also allows for ready comparison of what different people have independently said.

Source: Anonymous

Example So2: *Seeking feedback*

Source: Law 1977

		Self-assessment	Write the names of your other assessors here				
		1	2	3	4	5	6
1. Careful	Careful — tries to avoid mistakes, large or small						
	Thorough — sees a task right through						
	Gives attention to detail						
	Takes pride in work						
	Perfectionist — does not like to see a badly-done job						
	Concentrates closely						
2. Co-operative	Co-operative						
	Loyal — will not let friends down						
	Polite — does not like to offend anyone						
	Responds well to other people's suggestions						
	Adaptable — can fit in well with others						
	A 'joiner' — clubs, projects, anything that is going on						

This self-assessment is designed to be used in conjunction with classroom work. It is framed on the nine personal and social dispositions set out in the input section in the chapter 'Telling What?'. Students rate themselves on each feature (the rating method is flexible and students can add more descriptions). But students are also invited to go in search of others who know them, to see how they agree and disagree with the self-assessment.

Example So3: *Portrayal by 'adult other than teacher'*

Name .... Date ....

Placement .... Type ....

Over the past month Richard has given great service and support to me during my illness, he has shaved me daily in a most able manner and many other things too many to mention here he has a very special attitude to the elderly.

Trainee ☐
Supervisor ☐
Staff ☐
T. Leader ☐
Other ☐
Resident ☐

Comment pads record achievement in an immediate and informal way. The pads have an adhesive edge, and are stuck into the record at the student's discretion.

Source: Scottish Vocational Preparation Unit 1982

Example So4:   *Peer assessment*

A group of students were discussing the ability of one lad to stand up for himself. It developed into a group assessment session where adjectives were chosen and students and tutors assessed themselves and the other members of the group using several adjectives: e.g. confronter, leader, honest, loving, strong . . . A grid was drawn up for each one — sometimes the individual voiced his or her self-assessment first to clear the way for other comments.

Characteristic — leadership (x = positive)

e.g. *Raters*

		Diane	Kevin	Robert	Albert	Trevor	Sheila	Kate
	Diane		x	x	0	x	0	x
	Kevin	x		0	0	x	x	x
Subjects	Robert	x	0		x	x	0	0
of	Albert	0	0	0		x	0	0
Ratings	Trevor	0	0	0	0		x	x
	Sheila	x	0	0	0	x		x
	Kate	0	0	0	0	x	x	

From the grid the students learned a lot about how others see them.

Source: Scottish Vocational Preparation Unit 1982

EXPLORATION

Second thoughts on sampling

Contributor involvements

The underlying principle of sampling is to find people who are best able to portray what is needed to be known. That may mean asking for contributions from outside the conventional range of contributors to documents like school reports and cumulative records. It may mean asking people to speak of what they know — but have never been asked to speak of before. It may also mean not asking people who expect to be asked. All of this requires that they have new sampling procedures explained to them — their purposes and their processes (see Chapter 7, Proceeding with Caution?).

In any event people should clearly not feel obliged to contribute what they feel they cannot validly contribute. On pre-structured formats that might involve arranging for items to be coded to make it clear that a non-response means that the source has decided to say nothing about this matter — avoiding the danger that a non-response will be interpreted as meaning that the student is being rated as not possessing this particular quality or characteristic. The advantages are obvious of keeping different sources of information and impression about students separate from each other during the collection phase. People are influenced by seeing the opinions of others.

Collation

A central problem for sampling is collation. Asking contributors to make portrayals on separate slips, independently from each other, will increase the chances that a diverse — even contradictory — range of portrayals will be gathered. The wider the range, and the more diverse the contributions, the harder it is to scan the information and to reconcile it to a few simple sentences. This is as much an argument for as against wide and independent sampling.

Some methods of collation, particularly for summative purposes, seek to compact a range of statements into a manageable form. This usually means putting the statements side by side and making a judgement as to which is most representative of the student. Some methods, such as Sc3, provide a computer program to assist teachers with the task of collating and selecting information. Others, such as P5, program a computer to incorporate a varied range of statements into a single discursive account. Others take separate written and oral accounts and collate them by a process of discussion, which in the case of P8 and its associated system Co1, includes discussion with the student. Yet others allow for separate statements about students to remain separate on the record, such as Sc1, Sc2, and Co1. But such diversity of information does not always survive to the stage where the record becomes public, perhaps because it is feared that too much variation in the account will prove unmanageable to the reader. An exception is Sc5 which presents what might be called a 'multiple-histogram' of portrayals, showing how different contributors agree and disagree with each other concerning their pictures of the student. Some systems which are intended, in part, to become a public record nonetheless avoid any attempt systematically to select, analyse and collate material; they present 'raw' reports as complete and free-standing accounts of what the students have to say about themselves — Ss13 and Co2 are examples (see also the discussion of unreferenced portrayals in Chapter 4, Compared to What?).

The problems of collating a single and manageable portrayal of a student from a variety of sources is greater for summative than for formative intentions. Much of the material reproduced in this chapter is not intended to be addressed to anyone but the student. They lend themselves to the development of a folder which the student maintains as a source of feedback and reflection upon him or herself; and from which he or she will disclose (in discussion with teachers, in class, or on a more public written record) whatever he or she chooses to disclose (see also the discussion of student-maintained records in Chapter 7, Proceeding with Caution?). Selecting, co-ordinating and integrating that material into a usable form is — in such use of the material — work for the student to do.

Separate slip systems like those described in examples Cn1 generate a great deal of paper. in one school the tasks of deciding who was to be asked for reports, of distributing, collecting and collating the papers, were given to the students to carry out in class. It meant that the whole programme of sampling colleagues was seen essentially as feedback to students. It catalysed contact between subject teachers and students concerning their progress and behaviour at school — and concerning what that meant to them. It also involved students as active participants in the process of assessment rather than as passive recipients of other people's assessments received from a distance. The whole process was monitored by a tutor who was available to students to ensure that they knew how to assemble the material, and had someone to talk with concerning how it was coming out. The fact that it also relieved teaching staff of a great deal of logistical and clerical labour was a side-effect of the process.

Self-portrayal

It is commonly reported that when students are first invited to use self-portrayal methods like those set out in the Ss series above they experience difficulty. Part of the difficulty is reported to be an unease about portraying positive features about self, in a way which others may feel is arrogant or which might lead people to expect too much from them. Part is reported to stem from anxiety about putting anything on any kind of record which others will see as negative information about self. You may find your students at least as reluctant to rate themselves 'high' as to rate themselves 'low'. In both cases the problem is ameliorated where students can trust the people who will see what they risk disclosing; and where they can trust undertakings concerning the confidentiality of the material.

But part of the explanation is in the lack of practice we have given our students in making informed, considered and articulate statements about themselves. School and college curricula are largely exercises in cultural transmission; directing attention to cultures which are external to the students — their histories, dispositions, technologies, beliefs, values and so on. There is no necessary opportunity in them for students to engage in reflection, contemplation and introspection concerning their own individual histories, dispositions, skills, beliefs, values and so on. Where that is so people will have learned that their student-role is to *be told* how it is, not to *tell* how it is. A first shot at anything a person is unused to doing is likely to be gauche: more so where teachers (often involuntarily) control and manipulate what it is possible for students to say.

It seems unlikely, in any event, that introspection is ever entirely a pure reflection upon self. Much of what we say about self is made up of material that we first gained from direct and personal contact with other people; as models and as sources of feedback. A sense of personal identity is influenced by modelling; the recognition in others of qualities which are admired and therefore imitated or rejected and therefore avoided. It is also influenced by feedback; the acceptance of what others say about self. Students returning to school or college from (say) a work experience placement will often informally report in terms of people they have met and admired, or in terms of people who have told them something new about themselves. The more diverse the direct and personal contacts they make the more choices they have in the formation of a sense of personal identity.

The So series in this chapter makes fuller use of modelling and feedback than does the Ss series. But both ranges of methods could be extended to invite young men and women to identify and articulate the dispositions, skills, beliefs, values they have encountered in other people as models, and to identify and articulate what they have received from other people as sources of feedback. Examples like Ss9 and Ss10 could be extended or developed to refer to 'people met', 'what they are like' and 'what I learned about myself from them'. Such a process should of course be critical (*why* do you so admire this?' and *why* do you accept or reject what you were told?') but it would have the effect of equipping students with some of the basic language and concepts required for self-portrayal.

When it comes to a process of reflecting upon what specific learning has come from a particular part of the school or college programme, as it does in examples Ss7, Ss8, Ss9 and Ss10 and Ss13, teachers sometimes report that students have difficulty in saying much about 'new skills' they have learned. Where the process of reflection occurs several days after the event they experience even more difficulty. Where the process of reflection is carried out in conversation with (say) a pastoral care teacher who was not even present at the event, the difficulties can prove insuperable. Students can often report what happened, and what they did, but they cannot say in specific terms what they gained from the activity. This is sometimes because nobody ever told them what they were meant to gain — the activity was just presented as something to be done. The consequences for the techniques of self-portrayal are obvious. If students are to be able to articulate to themselves what they are gaining from their school and college experience, then they need to know at some point in each activity what they are supposed to be gaining from it; and they need an opportunity to reflect upon that at the time, and with the people most concerned. The consequences for syllabus and lesson design of introducing any workable programme of self-portrayal of learning are quite demanding upon the people concerned and upon their time.

In some cases the cues to reflection given in self-portrayal logbooks are a simple series, page-after-page, of repeated questions — Ss10 is an example. Apart from the difficulties of identifying learning and risking disclosure, the task of using such pages promises to be boring. Some methods invite students to choose the questions they want to use in relation to each activity — as does the logbook in P8. But the Ss and So series contain a varied range of methods for self-portrayal and seeking feedback. And even that diverse range of methods is capable of extension and development. There may be a good case in some programmes for providing an off-the-shelf collection of self-portrayal methods that can be selected and adapted by the students to portray what they find in themselves as a consequence of each experience, different students using different methods for different experiences. Some students in some activities may need the sort of structuring of their responses which examples Ss7 and Ss9 illustrate; the same students might prefer to report themselves more discursively in other activities — for example in the way suggested in examples Ss13 and Co1. There is, in this book, an extremely varied range of structured, semi-structured and loosely structured techniques of portrayal (for a full analysis see Chapter 7, Proceeding with Caution?).

What is obvious is that, if students are to be engaged in any educative process of self-portrayal, it is not going to occur because we provided them with some pieces of paper on which to write things about themselves.

ACTION

Planning a sample

You might now be in a position to take any system that you are adapting to your intentions, and to ask yourself the question 'who is in the best position to provide which parts of this portrayal?'.

In so doing you might want to consider the following:

- There may be more than one person whom you can ask to contribute to the portrayal of any particular feature of the student — some skills, for example, are cross-curricular and reveal themselves differently in different times and places and to different audiences and observers.
- You may want to take advantage of the opportunity for sampling in a variety of settings, in various sorts of activities inside and outside the school or college.
- You may want to link the formation of the portrayal to opportunities to meet the student and talk with him or her face to face; and/or to incorporate opportunities for reflection into classroom activities (say in the pastoral care or social education programme in the school or college).
- You may want to involve the student as a key source of information about him or her self: but if you decide to do that you will need to take account of the need for support and help for the students and any people they will consult in carrying through their part of the self-portrayal.
- You will need to think about how the different perspectives are to be collated into a manageable account for any public use you intend.

The task is to take the plan or example, or any part of it, and to revise and re-address its format so that it can be used by a wider range of contributors.

- Because wide-sampled information is likely to be quite penetrating and comprehensive you will have some ethical decisions to make concerning the control of the information (see Chapter 7, Proceeding with Caution?). There is a decision to be made about the extent to which the student should be involved as a collector and collator of that information; as custodian of the developing folder or file; and as controller of the use that is made of any material which emerges.

CHAPTER SIX

WORD PERFECT?

This chapter is designed to help examine:

- methods for reducing the effects of personal bias in portraying students;
- methods for maximising the effect of evidence, and minimising the effect of hunches and guesses;
- methods for improving the chances that what is received by the user is what is intended by the portrayer;
- methods for increasing the probability that the portrayal is about the student, not about the portrayers.

All forms of profiling rely upon the use of language, although some have experimented with the use of symbols as substitutes for language. The selection of words to convey meaning on a profile is a problem. It is a problem for designers where the profile is based on pre-arranged forms and structures, such as those which use criterion referencing. The problem for language is to avoid subjectivity.

Two forms of subjectivity are considered here. In one form the words do not mean the same thing to the portrayer and to the user. From the mind of the portrayer they are intended to convey one thing; to the mind of the user they convey something else. They are *unreliable* words and distort the transmission of material (see Chapter 2, Profiling Profiles, concerning reliability). In the second type the portrayer is saying what he or she intends, but it is at least as much about his or her own preferences and attachments as about the student. As we shall see, some uses of words collude with that possibility. A test for the second type of subjectivity is, 'would another person — with a different set of preferences and attachments — who observed the same behaviour have said the same thing?' If the answer is 'no', the portrayer is putting 'noise' into the communication system — it is noise because it is not about the student but about something else. The words are *invalid* and contaminate what is being transmitted (see Chapter 2, Profiling Profiles, on validity).

The skilled use of language in designing portrayals is therefore twofold: employing words (1) which permit sources to say what is intended, and not something else; and (2) which permit them to say what is about the student and not somebody else. Successful use of such skills will mean that what appears on the profile is reliable and corresponds validly with some reality.

ACTIVITY

Me and my words

This is an exercise which you can do alone, or — by photocopying page 152 — with other people. If you are going to work with others note now that you will be asked to portray people you know, and the exercise can be more useful if some of the people chosen are agreed by all members of your group. The people you choose to portray could be politicians or media personalities, but they could also be people you all know personally. They must be people you can portray by using some of the words on page 130. Pick at least two personalities; make at least one somebody you like or admire, and somebody you don't like or admire so much.

There are a number of distinct stages in the exercise; don't read on or compare your responses to anyone else's until you have completed the fourth stage.

First stage: Like me All of the words on page 130 have been used by teachers to describe students. Do any of them describe you?

- Which words would you use to describe yourself? Write the letter 'M' for 'me' over each one.
- Which are unlike you? Write 'U' for 'unlike me' over each one.

Second stage: I like Are there some human characteristics that you like or admire better than others?

- Which of the words describe characteristics that you admire or like to see in people? Write 'OK' over each one.
- Which do you not like or admire? Write 'N' for 'not liked' over each one.

Third stage: Like them Think of the personalities you have chosen to portray in this exercise. Using any of the words on page 130 (marked and unmarked), which ones apply to whom?

- Which words would you use to describe somebody you like and admire? Write an initial to represent that person over each such word.
- Which of the words would you use to describe somebody you don't like and admire so much? Write another initial above each word.

You can repeat this stage for other people you know.

Fourth stage: Associations Forgetting the people you have portrayed, pick out key words on the sheet, words which are particularly significant descriptions in the sense that they are things which, for you, it is important to know about a person. They may be important in a positive or negative sense.

- Circle one such word and see if you can identify others on the sheet which go with it, in the sense that you would think it likely that if the one thing were true of a particular person then the other thing would probably be true as well. Connect those words to your first word with lines to make a star. Your star has a key word at the centre and associated words at its points.
- You can choose other key words, negative ones and positive ones, and make other stars — in different colours to help separate them.

adaptable   adult   adventurous   aggressive   aloof   ambitious
amenable   antisocial   anxious   argumentative
artistic   Asian   assertive   boisterous   carefree   careful
careless   changeable   charming   cheerful   cleanly dressed
competitive   confident   considerate   consistent   conscientious
conventional   cool   co-operative   courteous   creative
critical   demonstrative   dependable   discontented
disruptive   doesn't wear school uniform   dominant in groups
dreamy   drifts   easily distracted   easily discouraged   easy-going
effusive   energetic   enthusiastic   extrovert   firm
flexible   fluent   follower   good attendance   gregarious
has flair   helpful   I like him or her   imaginative   impulsive
inattentive   intelligent   introvert   inventive
irresponsible   isolated   keen   leader   leaves tasks uncompleted
lively   long hair (boys)   loutish   mature   methodical
modest   moody   needs supervision   negative
nervous   no tie (boys)   obese   often absent   outspoken
passive   persuasive   placid   pleasant   polite   popular
private   proud   punctual   questioning   quiet   reads widely
rebellious   reliable   religious   resilient   reserved
resourceful   restless   satisfactory   seeks limelight
self-assertive   self-confident   self-indulgent   self-sufficient
sensible   sensitive   short   shy   sociable   solitary
sportsperson   strong personality   stubborn   studious
tactful   takes initiative   takes pride in work   talkative
tall   thorough   tidy   timid   too much makeup
tries hard   troublesome   unco-operative   unfriendly
unpredictable   unreliable   untidy   untrustworthy
very strong personality   West Indian   witty   works hard
works well without supervision

Fifth stage: My subjectivities? You have made associations and disassociations on the sheet:

- with yourself;
- with your preferences;
- with personalities you know;
- between words as descriptions of personality.

It is probable that some patterns exist which link one or more of these associations together. Can you spot any? There may be some overlaps between the way in which you have done one stage of the exercise and others. Working back through the stages: Is there any reason to say that the way you link descriptors together is bound up with the way in which you have portrayed the personalities? That either is bound up with what you like and admire — or don't? And that any is bound up with the way you see yourself?

Of course, any such binding together of words may be perfectly valid. But comparing your stage-3 portrayal and stage-4 star-formations with colleagues may suggest that there are some ways of talking about people which, valid or not, are particularly your own. The extent to which that is so, and the extent to which they have their roots subjectively in your personal preferences and your sense of your own identity is your own affair: until, that is, you begin to use the same associations to make portrayals of students that other people are going to read.

This exercise has been designed to suggest the existence of personally held mental constructs, to suggest the possibility that such constructs can lead to labelling and halo effects; and that stereotyping may have part of its roots in such processes of thinking. One word which encompasses all four phenomena is 'bias'. There are some types of word which positively invite biased portrayal.

INPUT

Bias

The urge to bind clusters of perceptions into pattern or *constructs* is a well-documented human characteristic. Constructs help us to make sense of what otherwise would feel like a random and unmanageable bombardment of our senses with disconnected bits of information. We haven't got time to examine critically every impression that comes piling in, so we keep our heads tidy by accepting unchecked associations as 'probably true'; fitting newcomes on that bit of our mental furniture which is already in place for that piece of 'information'. On that basis people have been known to have ready-made and labelled chairs for 'the BBC', 'nationalised industries', 'politicians', 'trade unions', 'the royal family', and 'teachers'. Constructs not only organise information, they provide a basis for anticipation: some people think they know what to expect from teachers. Sometimes, of course, such bases of expectation are valid; but not always. Yet people will sometimes deny the evidence of their own senses in order to maintain the familiar arrangement of their mental furniture. The mentally rigid are particularly prone; for them an alternative arrangement may — literally — be unthinkable. But nobody is utterly rigid, and history provides examples of persistent people who have persuaded others to think the unthinkable. We need constructs, but they can be changed.

Where constructs are about human personality they may form on a basis of what is felt to be 'like me' versus 'unlike me'; or on the basis 'I like or admire' versus 'I don't like or admire'. Such a construct would cause a person who has met somebody who is like him or her in some respect to believe that they are alike in other respects. Or it would cause a person who found another admirable in some respect to attribute other admirable characteristics to that person. Converse forms also occur, attributing to people 'not like me' or 'not admired' characteristics. There are other bases for attribution, but in all cases the assumption is that because one thing is true of a person then it is 'probably true' that another is also true. The arbitrary attribution of characteristics to a person is called *labelling*. One frightening possible outcome of labelling is that negatively labelled people convince their portrayers of their own perceptiveness, by tending to comply with the label. But not all labels are negative.

The effect is observable in groups and institutions as well as between individuals. Where a group develops a joint sense of what is admirable or contemptible, or of what is appropriate to or not appropriate to 'the likes of us', then the labelling process is mutually supported and reinforced. Students do it, so do teachers. It takes some independence of mind to attribute a negative characteristic to somebody that other members of the group agree is admirable or very much 'our kind of person'. Where such independence of mind is not exercised the resulting group labelling is called the *halo effect*. It is the group celebration of all virtue in a person who has shown evidence of only some virtue. There is also a converse (horns and tail?) effect.

Where such processes of labelling get institutionalised into the conventional wisdom of a group concerning a group the process is called *stereotyping*. It is one of the most pernicious and hard-to-deal-with sources of invalidity in profiling students, because profiling is an institutionalised process. One of the more fearsome consequences stems from that fact that institutions, including schools and colleges, tend to celebrate narrow ranges of preferred characteristics: in some organisations competitiveness will be valued above co-operation, in others sensitivity above aggression. Where such 'sheep' and 'goat' characteristics are readily identified, marginal reinforcement of an impression will perpetuate it. So that knowledge that a person is (say) black and talkative, or (say) female and quiet, or (say) long-haired and male, will support the belief that such people are also (say) aggressive or hostile, (say) sensitive or passive, (say) unco-operative or rebellious. That has only to be said for you, and everybody around you, to realise its invalidity.

The trouble is that constructs, labels, halos and stereotypes get used without us ever realising what has happened — the challenging question doesn't get asked. It is short-cut thinking; it survives best in the heads of short-cut thinkers — which is, because we need constructs, all of us!

Value-laden language is, you may have noticed in the last activity, particularly suitable to the purposes of labelling, the halo effect and stereotyping. Value-laden language conjures up impressions of what is:

- 'liked' versus 'unliked';
- 'admired' versus 'contemptible';
- 'like me' versus 'not like me';
- 'the likes of us' versus 'not the likes of us'.

Or, to put it another way, 'sheep' versus 'goat'! A useful tool for criticising the design of profiles is to question the extent to which their use of language invites the biased attribution of 'sheep-like' and 'goat-like' characteristics.

ACTIVITY

Checking the language

Below are examples of portrayals which have appeared on profiles and other systems intended to convey information about students in schools and colleges.

How trustworthy do they seem to you? Would you say that any are sufficiently free of the dangers of subjectivity that you could be reasonably sure that they convey some objective reality? Are there some that would arouse in you suspicions of subjectivity?

- Tick any that seem trustworthy to you.
- Cross any that don't.
- Are there identifiable differences between the ticked ones and the crossed ones?
- Can you agree any such characterising features with colleagues — and the examples to which those features apply?

' . . . is well mannered and courteous.'
' . . . needs constant encouragement to relate to others.'
' . . . has one or two particular friends.'
' . . . is an intelligent and amusing conversationalist.'
' . . . can use an index, such as a telephone directory.'
' . . . can take initiative, but prefers guidance.'
' . . . has outstanding self-confidence.'
' . . . has a very strong personality'.
' . . . is in the top 5% of a normal group of CSE candidates in English.'
' . . . is careful — tries to avoid mistakes, large or small.'
' . . . is a 'joiner' — of clubs, projects, anything that is going on.'
' . . . is absent regularly, but apparently with good reason.'
' . . . has identified and assessed the nature of specific environmental problems.'
' . . . is very polite and creates a good impression.'
' . . . can achieve basic tasks, such as making tea, under supervision.'
' . . . can understand the four rules of number with confidence.'
' . . . has a helpful friendly attitude.'
' . . . rarely participates in lessons.'
' . . . can use routine hand tools.'
' . . . can communicate adequately at conversation level.'
' . . . makes constructive and acceptable contributions in working with others, and has leadership potential.'
' . . . usually prefers to avoid limelight.'
' . . . is exceptionally resilient, copes easily under stress.'
' . . . is capable of mature friendships.
' . . . can consider simple problems, understand clear instructions and consider what action to take in simple situations.'
' . . . has distinct management ability.'

'. . . has not much co-operation, and there are some doubts about dependability.'
'. . . is lazy and uninterested.'
'. . . can understand and use the decimal system in everyday situations.'
'. . . knows the general properties and uses of common engineering materials.'
'. . . is reluctant to try new ideas.'
'. . . can carry out simple money transactions.'
'. . . has difficulty interpreting interpersonal behaviour, and modifying own responses when necessary.'

You can, of course, also use this exercise on any of the examples of profiling given earlier in this book or that you have from other sources.

INPUT

Speaking of subjectivity

All of the types of statement described below can give rise to a situation where what the reader receives is different from what was intended by the portrayer; or where what the portrayer intends to communicate is different from what the student is like. You may not agree that the examples given are the worst offenders in these respects. What you may agree is that it is virtually impossible to make any kind of interesting or even useful statement about anybody which is not liable to at least a couple of the criticisms of language outlined below.

Undefined statements say something which, although understood by the portrayers, may not be understood by its readers. Examples include: words which are not common coinage; words used with specialised connotations which may not be understood by other people; and words which are part of the technical vocabulary of education.

'. . . can understand the four rules of number with confidence.'
'. . . has identified and assessed the nature of specific environmental problems.'
'. . . has difficulty interpreting interpersonal behaviour and modifying own response when necessary.'

Mixed statements say more than one thing at a time. They are often attempts to portray people in as subtle a way as possible — taking account of the complexity and contradictions of human personality. But they can leave the reader wondering which part of the statement he or she is supposed to be paying attention to.

'. . . can take initiative, but prefers guidance.'
'. . . is absent regularly, but apparently with good reason.'
'. . . is an intelligent and amusing conversationalist.'

Non-operational statements, although apparently based on observation, employ language which cannot readily be used by the reader to conjure up an image of the behaviour observed. This means that another observer might use the same words to refer to quite different behaviour. It also means that the reader might conjure up a different image of what the portrayer is trying to convey.

> ' . . . is very polite and creates a good impression.'
> ' . . . has distinct management ability.'
> ' . . . has a very strong personality.'

Generalised statements portray features of human personality as though they apply to the person in all respects and circumstances. It is rarely possible for one person to make such a statement of another — we see so little of each others' lives. In some cases the only person qualified to make such a statement would be the student him or herself.

> ' . . . is reluctant to try new ideas.'
> ' . . . usually prefers to avoid the limelight.'
> ' . . . needs constant encouragement to relate to others.'

Interpretative statements do not pretend to be observations of behaviour, but point to underlying states. They frequently entail the use of abstract nouns. They are the kinds of statements that would require an intimate knowledge of the person being portrayed. In some cases the only person qualified to make such statements would be the student him or herself.

> ' . . . is capable of mature friendships.'
> ' . . . has outstanding self-confidence.'
> ' . . . is exceptionally resilient, copes easily under stress.'

Value-laden statements separate 'sheep' from 'goats'; expressing preference for this student — or identification with this student — rather than with other students. They invite bias, both in the portrayer's assessment and in the reader's response. At their worst they declare what is acceptable to the portrayers — without declaring what sort of person it is that such behaviour is acceptable to.

> ' . . . is lazy and uninterested.'
> ' . . . has a helpful friendly attitude.'
> ' . . . makes constructive and acceptable contributions in working with others, and has leadership potential.'

Some statements manage to combine a remarkably wide range of the six characteristics above with the use of remarkably few words. It is an easy criticism to make until we begin to consider the difficulty of avoiding those characteristics. If these are the 'vices', what are the 'virtues'? On these bases objective statements about students are those which are:

- *Defined* — everybody who reads them will understand them in the same way;
- *Singular* — they say one thing at a time;
- *Operational* — they conjure up clear images of people doing things;
- *Specific* — they say in what circumstances the characteristic has been displayed;
- *Guess-free* — they say what can be concretely known of the student;
- *Value-neutral* — they do not voice the portrayer's preference of one student above another.

It is a demanding list. It is not surprising to find, therefore, that objective portrayal, even writing criterion references, is honoured as much in the breach as in the observance. While total objectivity may be beyond our reach it is also possible that by paying attention to the sources of subjectivity we may be able to avoid its damaging effects. The above list adds more tools to the purposes of criticising profile design.

EXPLORATION

Second thoughts on language

'Had done', 'can do', or 'is like'?

Three basic forms are represented in the usages of language in profiling. The 'has done' form states that the student has been observed to do something — perhaps on only one occasion and in only one situation. ('Has done' statements include 'has shown that he or she knows' statements.) Such statements can most easily have the virtues of definition, singularity, operationalism, specificity, freedom from guesswork and value-neutrality.

But a user might need to know more. So, more commonly, 'can do' statements imply not only that the student has done it once, but can do it again — the bolder versions implying that it can be done in a variety of circumstances. The implication that the student has been seen to do it on a number of occasions in school or college — in a variety of circumstances and by a number of people — is not always supported by the evidence on which a statement is based. However some degree of generalisation to a single 'can do' from a number of 'has dones' may be supportable, particularly where users need to be able to anticipate what the student is going to be capable of in the future.

The step from 'can do' to 'is like' involves an even bolder interpretative venture. And when it comes to portraying dispositions and motives the dangers are considerable. The language of dispositions and motives is subtle, the meaning of words shade into each other, they refer to states rather than to behaviour, they tend to be generalised, they are frequently abstract nouns and they often invoke personal preferences and attachments. Yet, if it is possible to say that a person is 'cheerful', 'courteous', 'in need of constant encouragement', or 'has shown loyalty to the school on a number of occasions' one has said something very useful: because we are now portraying something of the inner roots of behaviour — and that can be useful to summative, formative and catalytic intentions. This is not to support the use of language which invites portrayers to make unsupported guesses about inner states, concerning which they can have no knowledge and into which they have no right to intrude. Some statements of the 'is like' type remain the sole property of the student — for him or her to disclose or not to disclose. It is difficult to argue, though, that no contributor, in any circumstance, on the basis of whatever wealth of verifiable evidence, should ever make some statements of the 'is like' type.

Value neutrality

Publicly used value-laden terms invite associations with preference and identification, and thus invite 'sheep and goat' labelling, halo effects and stereotyping. But avoiding value-laden terms is difficult. All terms of the 'has done' and 'can do' are value-positive in the sense that it is better to be able to do something than not to be able to do it. And almost all 'is like' abstract nouns are value-laden — at least in the sense that people have preferences concerning the nouns they like, or do not like, to be able to attach to people close to them. If the alternative to value-laden is value-free it is going to prove difficult to achieve. Almost all the words we use to describe ourselves have positive or negative values attached to them.

But the problem for value-laden language is at its most acute when a single range of possible portrayals polarises value-positive and value-negative terms. Look, for example, at example Cg4 on page 72. The 'A' and 'E' parts, you may agree, could entice a 'ticking and flicking' portrayer to label too easily a student with what is felt to be the probable truth that he or she is an 'A' type or an 'E' type.

Finding value-free ways of publicly portraying students may be difficult, but there is another possibility. It is to express all characteristics in value-positive terms, like portrayals of the 'has done' and 'can do' type. Criterion references — even hierarchically arranged — are usually written so that every statement made of a student describes a positive achievement, as examples Cc1, Cc3 and Sc5 illustrate.

A good many human dispositions — even some that are disapproved of in schools and colleges — are also capable of being stated positively. Indeed almost all the dispositions listed in 'What Might Go on a Profile' (page 59) can be voiced in *both* positively and negatively loaded terms. What is 'exceedingly co-operative and helpful' to some is 'obsequious' to others. What is 'resentful and unhelpful' to some is 'self-contained non-conformity' to others. The problem with Cg4 is not that the language is loaded — it is that it is value-polarised. By contrast example Cg2 appears to have made some attempt — not entirely successful — to put equal value-loading at both ends of each of its scales. It may, therefore, be much less likely to lead to 'sheep and goats' labelling. Value neutrality can be achieved by giving all terms a value-positive loading. A test of whether or not this is possible is to take an example — like the checklist in example So1 on page 120 — to see if every negatively loaded term there can be restated in a positively loaded way.

Public and private use

There are a number of arguments why the language which appears on a profile portrayal of a student should be positively loaded. (1) If it is not a statement of real and valued achievements it is unlikely to be used by the student for the purposes for which it is intended. (2) Value-negative terms, especially — but not exclusively — where they have to be chosen from a polarised list which also contain positive terms, invite labelling, halo effect and stereotyping. These arguments are stronger for public summative then for private formative profiling.

There is another argument: (3) negative feedback is difficult to handle. But, while it is true that hearing people say negative things about me is going to be painful, it can also be fruitful. A great deal depends who says it, with what intention, in what circumstances and in what tone. Setting up a system of student portrayal which only gives students positive feedback may amount to setting up a bland system of portrayal which will, in the eyes of the students themselves, eventually lose credibility. 'Bad news' about self delivered in the right way is grist to all our mills. So a system which, in the name of arguments 1 and 2, allows the *formative* part of any profiling system to deprive students of all such roughage to self-understanding may not be doing them as much justice as their capacity to deal with it deserves.

Using the language and other ways of minimising the effects of subjectivity

It is unlikely that any system of portrayal will be designed that is entirely free of the sorts of subjectivity examined in this chapter. It is, in some ways, a cost-benefit exercise: the design of a system which is entirely free of subjectivity may well prove so limited, trite and anodyne as to be useless for the purposes for which it was intended. The virtues of portrayal, like other virtues, should be used with intelligence — holding on to the 'goodness' for which they stand, but not allowing oneself to be uselessly hampered by their rules!

There are, however, other strategies which can be used to minimise some of the worst effects of subjectivity.

- Clearly state on the profile the context in which the portrayal is made. Profiles often incorporate statements of the curricula which the students have followed; what they do much less often is to state the school or college ethos in which that curriculum is set and in which this portrayal is being made. A few words about the sorts of values celebrated in a school, college or programme could — to the perceptive reader — be a useful means of understanding the statements that the school or college makes about its students.
- Collecting material from a range of sources of portrayal, particularly from people outside the school or college ethos, so that the inevitable subjectivities of one source stand the maximum possible chance of being diluted by the different subjectivities of another source. Involving the student her or himself in the process of collecting and reviewing material is an important elaboration of this principle (see Chapter 5, Says Who?).
- Keep sources separate from each other before they are collated into any portrayal, so that what one person says will not have a chance to influence another — setting up a halo effect.
- Staff-consultation and development activity in which colleagues are introduced to profiling well before it is implemented; given a chance to comment on any potential it contains for subjectivity; and alerted to the dangers of allowing such contamination to enter the system. (The adaptation of exercises in this handbook might provide part of such staff-development activity; see also Chapter 7, Proceeding with Caution?).

ACTION

Minimising subjectivity

Below are summary checklists of the main issues raised in this chapter. They are intended for use by groups wanting to re-jig any current system of portraying students in schools and colleges. One use of it would be to take the whole or a part of an existing system and see to what extent colleagues can agree about what sort of action, if any, should be taken.

About the language

- Should any of the material be rewritten so that . . .
  . . . what is meant is more clearly *defined*?
  . . . it contains *singular* statements, which say one thing at a time?
  . . . it conjures up *operational* images of people doing things?
  . . . it is *specifically* related to the circumstances in which the statements are made?
  . . . it is *guess-free*, avoiding inviting interpretations from contributors?
  . . . it is *value neutral*; by using value-positive terms avoids inviting 'sheep and goats' effects?
- Should any of the material be rewritten to make it clearer to the reader that what is being portrayed is . . .
  . . . what has *been done*?
  . . . what *can be done*?
  . . . what somebody is prepared to say the student *is like*?

About the structure

- Where difficulties are encountered on any of the above tasks, can they be helped by separating the portrayal into . . .
  . . . elements that are intended only for the student's *private* use?
  . . . elements which are intended for *public* use?

About the context

- Will any of the following strategies help:
  . . . a programme of consultation and staff-development with colleagues in the school or college?
  . . . a statement on the profile making it clear from what school or college ethos these statements are coming?
  . . . the use of a wider range of sources of portrayal?
  . . . the admission that there are some parts of a portrayal which only the student can make — if he or she chooses to do so?

Examples in this handbook that lend themselves to this as a task-group training exercise include:

- for *experience*: Cc4, Co1, Co2, Ss7, Ss8, Ss9, Ss11, Ss13.
- for *mental and physical abilities*: Cg1, Cn1, Cc1, Cc2, Cc3, Sc2, Sc3, Sc4, Sc5, Ss6, Ss10, Ss12.
- for *dispositions*: Cg2, Cg3, Cg4, Cn3, Sc1, Ss3, Ss4, Ss6, So1, So2.
- for *motives*: Ss1, Ss2, Ss5.

CHAPTER SEVEN

PROCEEDING WITH CAUTION?

This chapter is designed to help examine:

- methods for ensuring that portrayal procedures are ethically defensible;
- methods for selecting format structures and techniques which are useful to the purpose for which they are intended;
- methods for linking portrayal processes to the other processes of the institution, such as counselling, curriculum development and teaching and learning processes;
- methods for ensuring that the contributors and users of portrayals are involved in ways that they find manageable and valuable.

The issues raised by this handbook are not only about the *assessment* of students; they touch upon all the other issues for education and training — of *curriculum*, of teaching and learning *methods*, and (in this section) of *organisation*. Organisational tasks include ensuring that information and impression moves from contributors to users in an efficient, valid and usable form. But they also involve ensuring that the people to be involved in the portrayal — contributors and users — are involved in ways which they find valuable, manageable and defensible.

An ungraded CSE in history, some would agree, is like a 'failure'. But, even if it is, it is *merely* a failure in CSE history, because it is about one — rather small — part of the student's life. It is a moot point whether it is possible to 'fail' in the terms of any of the more manifest methods of portrayal described here; but it is possible to look 'better' or 'worse' — to self and others. If that is so for these more searching methods, then the ethical implications for their use are extremely severe. It is with the ethics of portrayal that this section begins.

ACTIVITY

Ethics of portrayal

Below is a list of statements, each of which raises an ethical issue concerning the portrayal of students. They are for your consideration and discussion with colleagues. But, before you do so, see to what extent you tend to agree or disagree with each statement. Each has a range of possible responses:

+3 you agree with the statement absolutely;
+2 you substantially agree with the statement;
+1 you tend to agree, more than disagree;
  0 you can't say;
−1 you tend to disagree, more than agree;
−2 you substantially disagree;
−3 you disagree absolutely.

Circle the response next to each item which most closely corresponds to your own feelings on that issue. For the moment ignore the scores (1–7) under each response, and ignore the boxes on the right. Don't agonise over it too much; give a 'gut' reaction. It is, in any event, a fairly crude device for measuring attitudes. It may prove more useful as a means of stimulating your own response to the issues, than as a scaled measure of them.

1. It is more important that portrayals should be useful to education decision-makers and recruiters than that they should be open to students.

   Agree   Disagree
   +3 +2 +1   0   −1 −2 −3   □ A
   7   6   5   4   3   2   1   □ E

2. Students should have the right to remove, correct, or add to what has been said about them.

   Agree   Disagree
   +3 +2 +1   0   −1 −2 −3   □ B
   1   2   3   4   5   6   7

3. The only information that should be made public about a student is positive information.

   Agree   Disagree
   +3 +2 +1   0   −1 −2 −3   □ D
   1   2   3   4   5   6   7

4. The only person who should decide what goes into his or her portrayal is that person her or himself.

   Agree   Disagree
   +3 +2 +1   0   −1 −2 −3   □ B
   1   2   3   4   5   6   7

5. Written information and impression about a person is that person's property — to show only to whom he or she will.

   Agree   Disagree
   +3 +2 +1   0   −1 −2 −3   □ C
   1   2   3   4   5   6   7

		Agree				Disagree				
6.	There are some things about students which, although the students may object, teachers should put 'on the record'.	+3 7	+2 6	+1 5	0 4	−1 3	−2 2	−3 1		B E
7.	Anything recorded or reported about a student should be available for that student to see.	+3 1	+2 2	+1 3	0 4	−1 5	−2 6	−3 7		A
8.	Nothing should be recorded or reported which might prove harmful to a student's interests or self-image.	+3 1	+2 2	+1 3	0 4	−1 5	−2 6	−3 7		D
9.	We should not hedge procedures with controls about who says what; it represents an unjustified distrust of teachers' integrity.	+3 7	+2 6	+1 5	0 4	−1 3	−2 2	−3 1		E
10.	If any disclosure is made from a record or report to anybody other than the student then that fact should become part of the record — and told to the student.	+3 1	+2 2	+1 3	0 4	−1 5	−2 6	−3 7		A
11.	However sensitive the information, there is always some part of it that a teacher can tell someone, some time; nothing can be utterly confidential to the student.	+3 7	+2 6	+1 5	0 4	−1 3	−2 2	−3 1		C
12.	Maintaining portrayals which students and parents can see is inviting more trouble than it is worth.	+3 7	+2 6	+1 5	0 4	−1 3	−2 2	−3 1		A
13.	Some people's needs for information about students are so important that the teacher must have the right to pass it on to them.	+3 7	+2 6	+1 5	0 4	−1 3	−2 2	−3 1		C
14.	A teacher noticing that a colleague has put unsubstantiated opinion on the record, should use every means to see that it is removed.	+3 1	+2 2	+1 3	0 4	−1 5	−2 6	−3 7		
15.	Portrayals are not just made in the interests of individual students — teachers have other purposes for information, and the content of the portrayal must serve those purposes.	+3 7	+2 6	+1 5	0 4	−1 3	−2 2	−3 1		B D
16.	Intentions for the use of the information should be made clear to students at every stage in the development of any record or report.	+3 1	+2 2	+1 3	0 4	−1 5	−2 6	−3 7		

17. An integrated programme of schooling, further education, training and entry to employment means teachers must be free to record and report students' 'strengths and weaknesses'.

Agree +3 +2 +1 0 Disagree −1 −2 −3 ☐ C
       7 6 5 4   3 2 1   ☐ D

18. Teachers must be free to set down any piece of information about a student — as long as it is factual.

Agree +3 +2 +1 0 Disagree −1 −2 −3 ☐ E
       7 6 5 4   3 2 1

The issues contained in the items are intended primarily to stimulate reflection in you, and discussion with your colleagues. But they can also be scored; and scoring will give a rough-and-ready basis for comparing your position on some of the issues with those of your colleagues. There is a basic 'score' and a series of cluster 'scores'.

Basic score. Each response has a score of between 1 and 7. Write your scores in the box on the right, and total them. You will get a total score between 18 and 126. You could use the scale below to plot your own score and the scores of your colleagues — if they choose to tell you.

```
├──┼──┼──┼──┼──┼──┼──┼──┼──┼──┤
  20  30  40  50  60  70  80  90  100 110 120
```

- Plot 'M' for 'my' score; two 'R's for the range of scores in the group; and 'A' for the average for the group.
- Higher than average scores *might* suggest a professional ethic based on a belief in the integrity of the school or college system, of the teachers who work in it, and of its partners in education, in training and elsewhere. Higher scores might also suggest an associated wish to minimise interference with what teachers — as professional people — do.
- Lower than average scores *might* suggest a professional ethic based on a commitment to the rights of students as individuals; rights to which all institutional, bureaucratic and professional interests must remain secondary. Lower scores might also suggest the associated wish to make the collection and use of information accessible to, and controlled by, the individuals it concerns.

Comparing 'scores' will give you a way of seeing where you come in relation to colleagues' opinions on such issues. (This, incidentally, is a normative comparison: see Chapter 4, Compared to What?). It might also provide material for an exploratory discussion with them of ethical principles embedded in the tasks of profiling.

Cluster scores. Getting a single score out of range of issues like those listed in the inventory is a bit like getting a single mark out of performance in a school or college subject. It might say something for normative comparison purposes, and if it can be discussed it can be more useful than that; but, as a global score, it obscures as much as it illuminates. For there is more than one sort of 'knowledge' represented in the list; and they can be separated and (in the literal sense) 'profiled'. There are five different clusters of items, each representing a different emphasis in the issues. Each cluster has four items, and yields a 'score' of between 4 and 28. The score boxes have been marked with letters which identify each cluster.

'A box' total

```
├───────────────┼───────────────┼───────────────┼───────────────┤
5              10              15              20              25
```

- Higher scores suggest support for *teachers' maintenance* of records, free of outside interference.
- Lower scores suggest support for *student and parent access* to records about students.

'B box' total

```
├───────────────┼───────────────┼───────────────┼───────────────┤
5              10              15              20              25
```

- Higher scores suggest support for the right of *teachers to decide what content is recorded*.
- Lower scores suggest support for the right of the *student in deciding what is recorded*.

'C box' total

```
├───────────────┼───────────────┼───────────────┼───────────────┤
5              10              15              20              25
```

- Higher scores suggest support for the *teacher's decision concerning who will make use* of the information for what purposes.
- Lower scores suggest support for the *student's decision concerning who will make use* of the information.

'D box' total

```
├───────────────┼───────────────┼───────────────┼───────────────┤
5              10              15              20              25
```

- Higher scores suggest support for uses of the information which may be *independent of the interests of individual* students.
- Lower scores suggest support for the use of information which are *exclusively in the interests of the individuals* to which it refers.

'E box' total

```
├───────────────┼───────────────┼───────────────┼───────────────┤
5              10              15              20              25
```

- Higher scores suggest support for the *integrity and responsibility of teachers* in maintaining records.
- Lower scores suggest that *teachers' powers in maintaining records should be curtailed*.

Comparing your own cluster scores may suggest that some aspects of that issue are more important to you than others. (This, incidentally, is an idiographic comparison: see Chapter 4, Compared to What?).

All the issues raised here are issues of control concerning who says what to whom. Whatever position you and your colleagues take on such issues, you may agree that the students have the right to be told on what basis material is going to be set down about them, by whom, and for whom.

INPUT

Whose control?

'Information,' it can be cogently argued, 'is power'. Planning procedures for the collection, storage and transmission of information about students entails decisions about who is to be in control of what.

- Who maintains and who has access?
- Who decides what is set down about students?
- Who decides to what uses it will be put?
- In whose interests is the material to be set down?
- Who is to be entrusted with the responsibility of making such decisions?

There are three roughly distinguishable answers to such questions.

Teacher-controlled systems

Examples:
    P3:   Students Personal Progress Record;
    P5:   School Leaving Profile;
    P7:   Certificate of Vocational Preparation;
    Sc3: Pupil Profile.

Features:

- They are frequently intended for *summative* purposes, although it is often recommended (and it is always possible) that the student is given early access to the developing record as a source of feedback.
- They are generally *shorter and easier to read* than other types of profile; in some cases taking the form of a certificate which might be sent at the time of applying for a position (thus becoming part of the 'shortlist' screening as well as the final selecting process).
- They generally *involve the collation by teachers* of information from a number of sources. The use of 'ncr' paper and computerisation has been used to eliminate some of the routine.
- The content of the profile is generally *fitted into a pre-structured series of headings, criteria and frameworks*.

Student-controlled systems

Examples:
    Co2: Student maintained record;
    So3: Portrayal by 'adult other than teacher';
    So2:   Seeking feedback;
    and examples listed in the series Ss1–12.

Features:

- They are frequently intended for *formative* purposes; as an incentive to achievement, or to help students articulate what they are learning and becoming, and what this suggests for their own future actions.

- It is sometimes suggested that the student keep the material to *take with him or her to a selection interview* (such documents are, therefore, much more likely to be part of the 'selection' than of the 'screening' process).
- Some of the materials are designed to stimulate discussion and exploration in *face-to-face, small group and classroom work*, or they can readily be adapted to be useful in that way.
- Much of the recording undertaken by students can remain confidential to them, to disclose or not to disclose as they see fit. They may be freer, therefore, to articulate to themselves something about their hopes and yearnings, needs and aspirations — their *motivations*.
- The resulting record is the student's responsibility and he or she will do all the work of collecting, collating and assembly. This means that the student *can seek out a diverse range of sources of feedback* on his or her characteristics and achievements from both inside and outside school.

Jointly controlled systems

Examples:
  - P1: Personal Achievement Record;
  - P2: First Year Home-Base Curriculum Profile;
  - P4: Profile Report and Statement of Achievement;
  - P6: Record of Achievement;
  - P8: Profile Folder;
 - Ss10: Self-assessment in school or college subject.

Features:

- Some are intended for summative purposes (although many are more suitable for the selection stage than the screening stage). Most are intended for formative purposes. All have *catalytic* potential — putting students and teachers into discussions which will raise questions about the usefulness of what the school or college is offering.
- The *balance of control* between teacher and student varies: in some cases the student initiates all entries; in some cases no statement can go on the record without the student's agreement; in others the student discusses entries with the teacher who retains final control. In some cases students can opt in or out of participation in the scheme.
- The degree of *integration between student- and teacher-contributions* also varies: in some cases they remain separate from each other — in different parts of the portrayal; in others they are joint statements agreed between teacher and student.
- In some cases the *student maintains a part of the record entirely within his or her own control*, and without obligation to show it to or to discuss it with anyone else; they are free to do so as selectively as they wish.
- In some cases the headings and structure of the student-maintained sections are designed to make them *a basis for entries on a public record or report*.

All these types of system are capable of incorporating features other than those associated with control. They may be developed:

- To produce a *continuously developing* — or, at least, repeated — portrayal of the student, beginning (in some examples cited above) in the first year of secondary education: or to produce a *snapshot* portraying the student at any one time in his or her life.
- To invite the portrayal of students *in their school or college* work and what is obviously closely associated with it: or to invite a *wider portrayal* in which students' personal and social behaviours and, even, their inner yearnings and aspirations may find a place (see Chapter 3, Telling What?).
- To invite portrayals from a *range of sources outside* the school or college (see Chapter 5, Says Who?): or inviting portrayals only from *inside the institution*.
- To invite *contact with students*; in interviews, group and classroom work; or to rely wholly on what can be transmitted *on paper*.
- To invite entries into a *structured format*, with headings, criteria and frameworks which cue responses and ease the process of making entries and reading the document: or to invite portrayals with as *little pre-structuring* of response as possible, so that people are free to write discursively.
- To relate the portrayal to a *particular subject or* programme, so that individual teachers and departments can develop their own approaches to portrayal; or to make a single interdependent system of *cross-curriculum* — and even extra-curriculum — portrayals.

EXAMPLES

Techniques of portrayal

Within the broad decision concerning teacher-maintained, student-maintained, or jointly maintained procedures, there are a number of other decisions concerning what specific portrayal techniques are to be incorporated into the design. There is a wide choice, as examples already given in this handbook illustrate. Below are analyses of those techniques.

The techniques are arranged in a rough-and-ready sequence:

- Beginning with the *more structured* techniques; employing pre-defined headings, criteria and frameworks into which the portrayals must be fitted:
- Ending with the *less structured* techniques; leaving room for discursive and exploratory portrayal.

Other apparent features of the techniques are suggested in coded entries on the right of the list. The codes refer only to the technique used to illustrate each point in the list. Some examples have more than one technique and therefore appear more than once on the list.

The reference number before each example indicates where it can be found in the handbook. ('P' numbers are in Chapter 2, Profiling Profiles; 'C' numbers are in Chapter 4, Compared to What?; 'S' numbers are in Chapter 5, Says Who?.)

Features

Y means 'Yes', this is a design feature of this example.

Uncoded entries can be used, or adapted for use, in more than one way. Some that are coded could be adapted to show the alternative feature.

Forced-choice checklists (choosing one response excludes others)

	Separate programme or subject portrayals; rather than an inter-dependent cross-curriculum school- or college-wide system	Involving *face-to-face or classroom contact with students*; rather than relying on written communication	Capable of *gaining impression from outside school or college*; rather than remaining institution-based	*Limited to school or college- or programme-related information*; rather than more broadly a portrayal	*Continuous or repeated*; rather than single 'snapshot'
P2: First Year Home-Base Curriculum Profile	Y	Y		Y	Y
P3: Student's Personal Progress Record	Y			Y	Y
P4: Profile Report and Statement of Achievement		Y	Y		
P6: Record of Achievement	Y	Y		Y	
Cg4: Graded scale					
Cn2: Normed scale					
Sc3: Pupil Profile				Y	
Ss12: Self-appraisal checklist					

Grid-type profiles (arrange criteria in categories and hierarchies)

P8:	Profile Folder		Y		Y	Y
Cc3:	Grid-arranged criteria				Y	Y

Histograms (presents information, literally, in profile form)

Sc5:	Grid-type profile and histogram				Y	

Card sorts (avoids necessity for form-filling)

Ss6:	Card sorts		Y		Y	

Open checklists (portrayers can choose as many items as they will)

P1:	Personal Achievement Record				Y	
P5:	School Leaving Profile				Y	
P6:	Record of Achievement	Y	Y	Y	Y	
P7:	Certificate of Vocational Preparation	Y			Y	
Cc1:	Criterion-referenced portrayal				Y	
Ss3:	Checklist of career problems		Y			
Ss7:	Self-assessment in school or college subject	Y	Y		Y	Y
So1:	Wide-sampling checklist			Y		

Scored checklists (responses can be quantified)

Ss3:	Check-list of career problems	Y			
Ss5:	Self-assessment of values and needs	Y			
So2:	Seeking feedback	Y	Y		
So4:	Peer assessment	Y			

Incomplete sentences (sentence 'stems' which invite completion)

	1	2	3	4	5
Ss9: Report of experience 'stems'		Y			Y
Ss11: Self appraisal 'stems'					

Questionnaires

	1	2	3	4	5
Ss2: Preparatory self-reviewing		Y		Y	Y
Ss10: Retrospective self-reviewing		Y		Y	Y

Diaries, time sheets and journals

	1	2	3	4	5
P3: Student's Personal Progress Record				Y	Y
P8: Profile Folder		Y		Y	Y
Co1: Jointly-maintained record	Y	Y		Y	Y
Ss8: Time sheet		Y		Y	Y

Semi-structured portrayals (spaces, with cues to stimulate responses)

	1	2	3	4	5
P2: First Year Home-Base Curriculum Profile	Y	Y		Y	Y
P4: Profile Report and Statement of Achievement		Y	Y		
P6: Record of Achievement		Y		Y	
P8: Profile Folder		Y		Y	Y
Co1: Jointly-maintained record	Y	Y		Y	Y

Unstructured portrayals (gives room for discursive account)

	1	2	3	4	5
P2: First Year Home-Base Curriculum Profile	Y	Y		Y	Y
P4: Profile Report and Statement of Achievement		Y	Y		
P6: Record of Achievement	Y	Y		Y	
Co2: Student-maintained record		Y	Y		Y
Ss13: Record of self-directed learning		Y			Y

EXPLORATION

Second thoughts on procedure

How much structure?

Decisions concerning the degree of structure — as between forced-choice checklists and unstructured space for discursive writing — will depend in part on purpose and content of portrayal. But there are other considerations. Although it is clearly necessary to allow as much freedom as possible for sources of portrayal to say what they know, some designs also acknowledge the need for a degree of structure. Contributors may be helped by having some indication of the sort of material sought, and the kind of thing that can be reported. And a format of profiling achievements which declares the criteria on which any public document is to be based has the additional advantage of making those criteria manifest to all who are involved — contributors, students and other users of the documents. The decision about structure is often a matter of balancing needed support with needed freedom (see also the discussion of unreferenced portrayal in Chapter 4, Compared to What?).

Consulting students

Although developers of formats for portrayal frequently consult others while developing their design, that consultation is not invariably very extensive. Local employers are more likely to be asked about what they want portrayed and how they would like to see it set out. Other people are less likely to be consulted. Yet a design which has been enthusiastically developed by a task group deeply interested in its purposes and problems can suddenly appear much less impressive when the first student is asked to use it. The case for piloting designs before they are finally adopted is obvious. But members of a development group could also consider bringing students in at a much earlier stage. One or more lessons given to information and consultation on the purposes and problems of profiling could be both an educative experience for students and a useful source of pre-pilot feedback to developers. Much of the material in this handbook could readily be adapted to such uses. Presenting ready-made design for students to use, with no opportunity for them to examine it and discuss it before they are expected to use it, can invite misunderstanding, abuse and, perhaps, rejection.

Overlap, duplication and conflict

Ideas of portrayal and self-portrayal incorporated into documents called 'profiles', 'records of achievement', 'records of experience' and 'student-centred reviews' are not new. All schools and colleges already have procedures for developing portrayals which incorporate at least some of their elements. Teachers working with UCCA applications, or helping students make 13+ choices, or offering careers guidance, may well have developed procedures for portrayal and self-portrayal. Subject teachers will invite students to reflect on and portray their experience and learning. Departments in the school or college may have developed their own procedures for monitoring, assessing and reflecting upon the learning with which they are concerned. Teachers running work experience programmes or other community-linked programmes may be using techniques to help students prepare for, and reflect upon, their use of such experiences. It is possible — even likely — that the introduction or development of procedures for portrayal which you and colleagues are promoting will overlap, duplicate or even conflict with existing activities. You may be about to invade somebody else's territory!

The larger, more complex and less internally communicating the organisation, and the more extensive and comprehensive your own plans, then the more likely it is that such internal overlap, duplication or conflict will occur. It is better to find out about that at the planning stage, while co-operation, mutual support, negotiation and accommodation can still be built into the development, rather than when procedures have become settled, and people begin to feel they must defend against all-comers the territory they have marked out.

It argues for letting colleagues know what you are proposing. You may, in the end, decide to go ahead independently of other initiatives: but it is usually better to do that in knowledge than in ignorance.

Information, support and involvement

All but the simplest of the systems set out in this handbook take time to understand. Many an apparently simple device has features which are subtle enough to be overlooked on cursory examination. That is why a good many of the systems are accompanied by explanatory material — often in the form of a short handbook — explaining why the system has been established, why it has been set out in a particular way, and how contributors and users can best handle it. Almost all such handbooks are addressed to teachers; some are addressed to employers; some to parents; a few to students. Some develop separate handbooks for different groups.

Material incorporated into such handbooks can give an account of its purposes, including what other means of portrayal it is, and is not, intended to supplement or replace. It can give an account of the basis on which the material is released (including any restrictions you may want to put on photocopying or storing information). It can explain how the information and impression is gained, and what limitations that places on the comprehensiveness and authority of the statements. Where grades, norms or criteria are being used they should be explained, giving examples of the sorts of observations which different statements represent. It can give guidance and suggestions to contributors, including, if you wish, suggestions about how interview and classroom work can be based on the use of the material to enhance its validity and improve its educative effect.

But there is a limit to the depth of understanding that can be taken off the page. There is no substitute for person-to-person and group consultation — at the development stage, in pilot use, and in in-service training as the demands of the system become clear. In consultation, piloting and training people will have ideas for modification of the system; and keeping the development of the system flexible for as long as possible will benefit it and acknowledge their right to influence what they are expected to use. Their involvement will give them part-ownership of the system. You may have to compromise some of your own ideas in order to concede that; so if you don't want to know what they think, don't ask. But the consequences of not asking may be that they will feel they are being made to carry your baggage. And that courts abuse.

ACTION

Planning procedure

You may agree that the task of planning profiling procedures rests upon arriving at agreement with colleagues on a number of principles:

- Where in the institution is the development to be *based*? In a particular department, or associated with a particular syllabus or programme? Or more broadly in the institution, requiring an interdependence between a number of colleagues and departments. Which departments and colleagues are, initially anyway, to be involved?
- What are the main *intentions*? In what respects are they summative? formative? or catalytic? (See Chapter 1 Intentions for Profiling.)
- Who is to *control* what aspects of the procedure? Is control to be in the hands of teachers? of students? or jointly shared between teachers and students?
- What *range of information* and impression about students is to be included? Is it to be about things closely associated with school- and college-work? Or to include extra-curricular material? (See Chapter 3, Telling What?)
- How widely will the profile draw upon *sources*? From within the institution? Or taking account of impressions and information that may be gathered from outside? (See Chapter 5, Says Who?)
- Is the profile to make a *single* 'snapshot' portrayal of the student at one particular point in his or her life? Or is it to present a developing record with *continuous* or repeated series of impressions?

Agreement about such issues will clear the ground for more detailed planning. Those decisions might usefully be considered in three phases:

- About *outputs*; who is to receive the material for what purposes?
- About *inputs*; who is to contribute what kind of material?
- About *process*; how is the material to be handled in its journey from input to output?

A useful way of mapping procedures is to develop a chart along the lines suggested below. (The chart is completed for example P4 in Chapter 2.) The time scale (from left to right) could be a term, a year or several years, yielding several time spaces in which to locate activity. A useful task-group activity is to pin up a large sheet of paper which members of the group can write on as ideas are developed. The skilful use of a 'Pritt Stick' or 'Blutack' will permit trial entries and revisions.

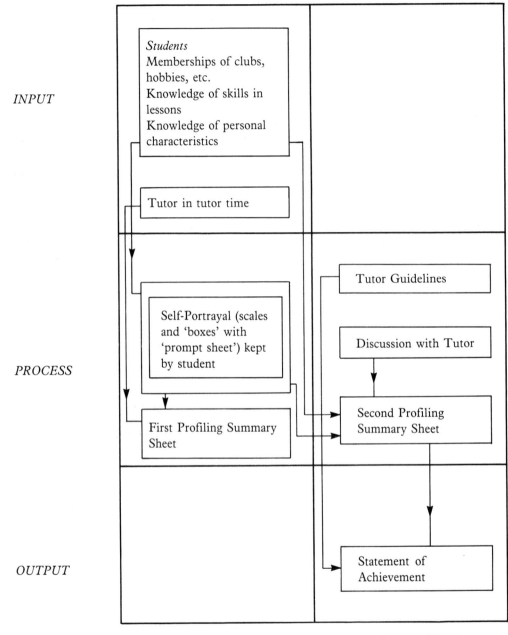

INPUT

PROCESS

OUTPUT

Students
Memberships of clubs, hobbies, etc.
Knowledge of skills in lessons
Knowledge of personal characteristics

Tutor in tutor time

Self-Portrayal (scales and 'boxes' with 'prompt sheet') kept by student

First Profiling Summary Sheet

Tutor Guidelines

Discussion with Tutor

Second Profiling Summary Sheet

Statement of Achievement

FOURTH YEAR   *FIFTH YEAR*

In the output section you could enter the points when people will need the material yielded by the portrayal: students, teachers, parents, outside 'recruiters', the careers service, and so on.

In the input section you could indicate the points where it would be possible and convenient to seek information and impression for the portrayal: from colleagues as individuals; from colleagues in case conferences; in classroom work with students; in face-to-face contact with students; through work experience placements and other such opportunities for gaining impression from outside sources; and so on.

In both cases setting it out in chart form will help to identify which contributors and users are being considered — and which are not, but who *might* be considered.

You have identified, between input and output, your opportunity to connect input to output — this is the *process*. One early decision is whether you want to do anything to advance input or retard output so that you have more time for process. The points that may prove to be among those you want to identify for process are where a particular technique could be useful; where material is separated into what can go on a public record and what can't; and where you know that some portrayal work is already being undertaken in the school or college, which could be adopted or adapted to your intentions.

It is not necessarily advocated that you use the resulting diagram to try to convey information about the proposals to anyone outside the group. It is likely to prove far too complicated for that. But your use of it should clarify your own thinking about procedures, and where those procedures need, and can, be supplemented and refined.

SUMMARY AND CONCLUSION

Profiling refers here to a range of alternative processes for portraying students in schools, colleges and training programmes. Their formats invite more explicit descriptions of students than do conventional formats. They are less subject-based in their framing. And they are as much concerned to convey an impression of how individual students go about learning as to convey an impression of what students have acquired from the content of learning.

Formats are means of saying what is known about students. Other parts of the process are concerned with knowing what is said about students. An important part of the process is, therefore, to develop formats which neither distort nor contaminate knowledge about students (see Chapter 1).

Although the term 'profiling' is used here to refer to the total process, not all formats are called 'profiles' — some are referred to as 'records of achievement', 'of experience', or 'student-centred reviews'.

A great deal of development work on formats has already been undertaken in schools and colleges throughout the country; and by organisations such as City and Guilds of London Institute, the Royal Society of Arts, and the Manpower Services Commission. But the professional responsibility for adopting, adapting and developing all the processes of profiling belongs to teachers — working individually, in subject departments, in organisation-based task groups, in in-service training programmes and other staff- and organisation-development activities (see the Introduction).

Alternative methods of portrayal are introduced for a variety of intentions. Those intentions may be developed from a comparison of unacceptable present realities and possible future ideals. Summative intentions include the intention to present for public use more detailed, cross-curricular, and rounded whole-person portrayals of students as they approach school-leaving. Formative intentions include the motivation of students, the provision to students of concurrent feedback on their performance, and their involvement directly in the educative tasks of self-portrayal and recording of experience. Catalytic intentions include the influencing of curriculum development, by assembling feedback on student performance to teachers, by providing materials to support teachers in their counselling roles, by developing criteria for portrayal which reflect and release (rather than control) curriculum development.

The relative importance of each of the intentions is a matter for decision-making in the individual schools, colleges and programmes. It is informed by a local appreciation of the significant shortfalls in more conventional methods of portrayal. It is often the case, however, that action taken on the basis of one set of intentions has unanticipated consequences in other areas of student and organisation development (see Chapter 1).

The content of information and impressions to be included poses technical problems. Some portrayals record events; some collate observations into more generalised statements concerning physical and mental skills and competencies; some attempt characterisations of students' personal and social dispositions; some portray student interests, motivations and drives. By no means all of what is portrayed in some formats is a direct concern of existing curricula. For some purposes it is important that the portrayal is not so arbitrarily restricted (see Chapter 3).

Bases for comparison also vary. Some use grades; some establish normative comparisons; some employ criterion referencing; some are more loosely structured. The latter methods are sometimes advocated because they minimise damaging and invalid comparison. But for some purposes, comparison between students is necessary, and some presentations of criterion-referenced portrayal invite between-student comparisons. Different purposes and different contents require different frames of reference (see Chapter 4).

Selecting sources of information and impressions represents another technical problem. Some portrayals are collections from subject teachers working to their own separate criteria; some sample and collate cross-curricular information and impressions from a range of teachers; some invite students to go in search of feedback throughout the school or college and outside it; some involve students in self-portrayal. The task of deciding who is in the best position to say what about a student is not a simple one: there are some aspects of student experience and personality which teachers are not in a good position to portray; there are some aspects which only the student is in any position to portray (what others must infer, students will often state — or, at least, imply). Wide sampling of sources of contribution to a profile entails more than circulating pieces of paper; contributors need help and support in making their portrayals. Self-portrayal by students can be a particularly demanding and stressful experience (see Chapter 5).

The use of language becomes a design problem where the portrayal is set out on a systematic and structured format. The use of negatively value-laden language in such layouts invites the stereotyping of students, and severely reduces the use of the portrayal for some (but not all) of its intentions. The use of language which invites the unverifiable attribution of ambiguously worded dispositions and attitudes to students, on the basis of a limited 'sample' of data and experience, are related and common problems for portrayal (see Chapter 6).

Procedural problems include those concerning the logistics of collecting, collating and disseminating information. Although most portrayals ultimately become the property of the student, some procedures are largely teacher-controlled; some assign a high degree of control to students; and some are designed to involve teachers and students in joint responsibility. In some cases, students retain parts of the portrayal in a folder for their personal use, releasing material for more public use at their own discretion. There are a variety of recording methods from which to select, ranging from scored checklists, through structured grid-type frames, to wholly discursive writing. Different types of information require different methods. Some methods are selected for their usefulness as counselling or classwork material. All such selections of method need to pay attention to the need to develop systems which can be readily managed by contributors to the portrayal, and readily understood by users. The selection of procedures sometimes, but not always, follows an extensive process of consultation with contributors to and users of the portrayals. Procedural issues uncover underlying questions concerning what is ethically defensible in the handling of information about individuals (see Chapter 7).

The adoption, adaptation or development of any process of profiling is often a more demanding task than is initially envisaged. Decisions and solutions which are likely to prove useful and acceptable in one school, college or programme may prove unacceptable and unworkable in another. Different solutions are, moreover, required for different intentions. The suggestion that a number of different types of approach should be piloted, refined and nationally co-ordinated is sensible.

With so much development work already completed there may be a temptation to adopt what has been developed elsewhere. Time is short, and gives edge to arguments for not re-inventing the wheel. But there is still plenty of room for further development; suggestions for such development are laid out in the 'action' sections in each of the chapters in this book.

After our ancestor had his (or her) first relatively successful shot at inventing the wheel, a second, third and fourth shot — we can safely assume — also proved necessary. Moreover, even when she or he managed to get the rim more or less circular and the axle more or less in the middle, there were still quite a lot of adaptations and further developments that could be made; and new applications that could be found. Profiling is at least as complicated in its workings as the wheel; and the possibilities for its use — and abuse — every bit as diverse.

APPENDIX

Publications

Balogh, Janet (1982) *Profile Reports for School-Leavers* (Schools Council Programme Leaflets). York: Longman.

Broadfoot, Patricia (1980) 'The Scottish Pupil Profile System', in Tyrrell Burgess and Elizabeth Adams (eds.) *Outcomes of Education*. London: Macmillan.

Corby Careers Office (1982) *Can Do*. Northampton: Education Committee.

City and Guilds (1983) *Profile Reporting System: Handbook*. London: City and Guilds of London Institute.

City and Guilds (1984) *Basic Abilities Profile* (pamphlet). London: City and Guilds of London Institute.

Crowley, A.D. (1983) *The Careers Problem Checklist: Manual*. Windsor: NFER-Nelson.

Further Education Unit (1982) *Profiles*. London: Further Education Unit.

Goacher, Brian (1983) *Recording Achievement at 16+* (Schools Council Programme Pamphlets). York: Longman.

Inner London Education Authority (1982) *Record Keeping and Profiling Guidance for Schools*. London: ILEA.

Law, Bill (1977) *Decide for Yourself*. Cambridge: Careers Research and Advisory Centre.

Manpower Services Commission (undated a) *Trainee Log Book*. London: Manpower Services Commission.

Manpower Services Commission (undated b) *Youth Training Scheme Log Book*. London: Manpower Services Commission.

Pearce, Barbara *et al.* (1981a) *Trainee Centred Reviewing on Youth Opportunity Programmes: A Guideline for Schemes*. Cambridge: Industrial Training Research Unit.

Pearce, Barbara *et al.* (1981b) *Trainee Centred Reviewing* (Research and Development Series: No. 2a). London: Manpower Services Commission.

Royal Society of Arts (undated a) *Vocational Preparation Courses: Clerical and Distribution*. London: Royal Society of Arts Examinations Board.

Royal Society of Arts (undated b) *Practical Profile Schemes: Communication Skills and Numeracy Skills*. London: Royal Society of Arts Examinations Board.

School Technology Forum (1984) *Pupil Profiles and Transferable Skills in School Technology*. Nottingham: National Centre for School Technology, Trent Polytechnic.

Scottish Council for Research in Education (1977) *Assessment System Manual*. Edinburgh: Scottish Council for Research in Education.

Scottish Vocational Preparation Unit (1982) *Assessment in Youth Training: Made to Measure?* Glasgow: Jordanhill College of Education.

Stansbury, Don (1980) 'The Record of Personal Experience', in Tyrrell Burgess and Elizabeth Adams (eds) *Outcomes of Education*. London: Macmillan.

Strathclyde Regional Council Education Department, Dunbarton Division (1979) *Clydebank EEC Project Teachers' Guide on Assessment*. Dunbarton.

Organisations

Bretton Woods Community School, Flaxland, Bretton, Peterborough.
Comberton Village College, Comberton, Cambridge.
Ernulf Community School, Barford Road, St. Neots, Huntingdon.
Evesham High School, Evesham, Worcestershire.
Marple Ridge High School, Buxton Lane, Marple, Stockport, Cheshire.
Norton Priory School, Castlefields, Runcorn, Cheshire.
The Springline Trust, The Mansion, Fore Street, Totnes, Devon.

COPYRIGHT ACKNOWLEDGEMENTS

We are grateful to those listed for their permission to use the following material in this book:

P1	Evesham High School
P2	Bretton Woods Community School
P3	Marple Ridge High School
P4	Comberton Village College
P5	Reproduced by permission from Schools Council Committee for Wales (1983) *Profile Reporting in Wales*, Cardiff.
P6, Ss7	Ernulf Community School
P7	Royal Society of Arts
P8	City and Guilds of London Institute
Cg1	Reproduced by permission of Strathclyde Regional Council Education Department.
Cg3, Ss1, Ss2,Ss9, Ss10	Reproduced by permission of the Manpower Services Commission from .Barbara Pearce et al (1981) *Trainee-Centred Reviewing* Research and Development Series: no. 2, London, MSC.
Cn1, Sc2	Reproduced with permission from Janet Balogh *Profile Reports for School-Leavers* (1982) (Schools Council Programme Pamphlets) York, Longman.
Cn3	Reproduced with permission from John Munro Fraser *Handbook of Employment Interviewing* (1982) London, FEU.
Cc3	Copyright Hertfordshire County Council
Cc4, Co1, Sc4	Reproduced by permission of the Further Education Unit, from *Profiles* (1982) London, FEU.
Co2, Ss13	Reproduced by permission of the Springline Trust

Sc3	Reproduced with permission from *SCRE Assessment System Manual* (1977). Edinburgh: Scottish Council for Research in Education.
Sc5	Reproduced with permission from School Technology Forum 'Pupil Profiles and Transferable Skills in School Technology' (1984). Trent Polytechnic, Nottingham, NCST.
Ss3	Reproduced with permission from T. Crowley *Career Problem Checklist* (1983), Windsor, NFER-Nelson.
Ss4, So3, So4	Reproduced with permission, from Scottish Vocational Preparation Unit *Assessment in Youth Training: Made to Measure* (1982) Glasgow, Jordanhill College of Education, SCOVO.
Ss5, So2	Reproduced with permission from B. Law *Decide for Yourself* (1977) Cambridge, CRAC.
Ss6	Reproduced by permission of Corby Careers Office. Developed by Northamptonshire County Council in conjunction with the Manpower Services Commission.
Ss9	Industrial Training Research Unit Limited is further acknowledged for initiating the idea of 'formative self-assessment' which led to the research.
Ss11	Norton Priory School.
Ss12	Reproduced with permission from Brian Goacher *Recording Achievement at 16+* (1982) (Schools Council Programme Pamphlets) York, Longman.

INDEX